# THE VISIT

# THE VISIT

## OBSERVATION, REFLECTION, SYNTHESIS FOR TRAINING AND RELATIONSHIP BUILDING

by

**ANNETTE AXTMANN, ED.D.**

and

**ANNEGRET DETTWILER, ED.D.**

·P A U L·H·
BROOKES
PUBLISHING CO.®

Baltimore • London • Sydney

**Paul H. Brookes Publishing Co.**
Post Office Box 10624
Baltimore, Maryland 21285-0624

www.brookespublishing.com

Typeset by A.W. Bennett, Inc., Hartland, Vermont.
Manufactured in the United States of America by
Versa Press, Inc., East Peoria, Illinois.

The photos in the center and lower right corner of the front cover are used courtesy
of Seth Kramer.

All illustrative vignettes are based on actual Visits. Names and identifying details
have been changed to protect privacy.

The red blocks recommended for the tasks in the Observation, Reflection, Synthesis Guides can be purchased separately in packages of 10. To order, contact Paul
H. Brookes Publishing Co., Post Office Box 10624, Baltimore, MD 21285-0624
(1-800-638-3775; 410-337-9580; www.brookespublishing.com).

**Library of Congress Cataloging-in-Publication Data**

Axtmann, Annette.
   The visit : observation, reflection, synthesis for training and relationship building /
by Annette Axtmann and Annegret Dettwiler.— 1st ed.
       p.    cm.
   Includes bibliographical references.
   ISBN 1-55766-808-6 (pbk.)
   1. Social work with children.   2. Maternal and infant welfare.   3. Child welfare
workers—Supervision of.   4. Family social work.   I. Dettwiler, Annegret.   II. Title.
HV713.A98 2005
362.7—dc22                                                                    2004026094

British Library Cataloguing in Publication data are available from the British
Library.

# CONTENTS

# ADVISORY BOARD
## FOR THE VISIT TRAINING AND DISSEMINATION PROJECT

**Lucille Echohawk, M.Ed.**
Senior Specialist
Indian Child Welfare/Casey Family Programs
6102 Cole Lane
Arvada, CO 80004

**Emily Fenichel, M.S.W.**
Editor in Chief
ZERO TO THREE Press
ZERO TO THREE:
    National Center for Infants,
    Toddlers and Families
2000 M Street, NW
Suite 200
Washington, DC 20036

**Tammy Mann, Ph.D.**
Director
Early Head Start National Resource Center
ZERO TO THREE:
    National Center for Infants,
    Toddlers and Families
2000 M Street, NW
Suite 200
Washington, DC 20036

**Rebecca Shahmoon Shanok, L.C.S.W., Ph.D.**
Director
Institute for Infants, Children and
    Families
Jewish Board of Family and Children's
    Services
120 West 57th Street
New York, NY 10019

**Cynthia Stringfellow, M.S.**
Director
Midwest Learning Center for Family
    Support
Family Focus
310 South Peoria Street
Suite 301
Chicago, IL 60607

# PREFACE

*The Visit: Observation, Reflection, Synthesis for Training and Relationship Building* originated at the Center for Infants and Parents (now known as the Rita Gold Early Childhood Center) at Teachers College, Columbia University. Families enrolled in the Center's service program for babies and toddlers enabled graduate students, acting as the Center's caregivers, and me (Annette Axtmann), the Center's director, to relate our observations to practice, developmental theory, and research. We reflected and garnered insights from our synthesis of what we were developing together. This integrative process is reflected in the Visit itself.

The Center for Infants and Parents opened in 1982. A meeting of the child, parent,[1] and director was required immediately after enrollment. During the meeting, we observed the child as he or she responded to developmental tasks. In 1983, we added observations of the parent–child interactions to the child's task performance and a reflective parent interview. By 1991, in-service training and teamwork had begun; the practitioner who worked most often with the family was participating actively during the family meeting and in a co-review with his or her supervisor following the meeting. The practitioner also participated in a conference with the parent after the Visit was conducted.

In 1994, the Center formed a team of graduate students and colleagues who documented a need in the field for an instrument such as the Visit (Rosa, 1996). We held a series of feedback sessions with directors of Early Head Start, group care directors, and directors of early intervention programs. These directors stressed the Visit's ability to uncover a hidden, suspected, or undiagnosed need for intervention with infants and their families. Some of these directors enabled us to conduct field trials in a wide range of service programs. During these trials, we added a follow-up letter for the parent, to be written by the Visit team as a culmination of the co-review. These trials secured parental feedback about what the experience meant and practitioner feedback about what was learned during use of the Visit.

By 1997, the Visit's development team had integrated the nonlinear dynamic systems theory for understanding development throughout all aspects of observation, reflection, and synthesis in the Visit. The Visit applied this theory directly to practice with very young children and their families. We drafted a description of the Visit and its Observation, Reflection, Synthesis Guides. Our Advisory Board reinforced prior advice from the field that the Visit meets the strong need for a framework that combines supervision with in-service training for direct care practitioners focused on the well-being of babies, toddlers, and their families. We hope that you have as much fun with the Visit as we have had through the years!

---

[1]The word *parent* is often used in this book to indicate the family member(s) participating in the Visit. Family participant(s) are unique to each child's situation and can be one or both parents, another family member, or a caregiver assigned to the family.

## DESCRIPTION OF THIS BOOK

The Visit fulfills an identified need for rigorous, ongoing supervision and in-service training, which are integral to service systems that care for the well-being of families with babies and toddlers. A description of the Visit is organized in six parts:

1. Introduction to the Visit
2. The Visit in Practice
3. Theory and Principles that Guide the Visit
4. In-Service Training for the Direct Care Practitioner
5. Role of the Supervisor
6. Benefits to the Service System

Also included are references; a glossary; an annotated bibliography; User Information for the Observation, Reflection, Synthesis Guides; Materials for the Tasks; and a Developmental Characteristics Chart.

The Visit description is accompanied by Observation, Reflection, Synthesis Guides (or "Guides"). The Guides are organized into eight age ranges: 2–4 months, 4–7 months, 7–10 months, 10–13 months, 13–18 months, 18–24 months, 24–30 months, and 30–36 months. Each Guide contains a detailed, photocopiable Visit Record, which contains directions, lists of age-appropriate tasks and materials, and reflective parent interview questions for the initial and subsequent visits. Instructions pointing the user to the Developmental Characteristics Chart are included as well. Central to each Guide are directions for the user to observe the child's behavior from a nonlinear dynamic systems perspective. The Future Supervision for Direct Care Practitioner Form is offered for listing practice goals. Printable versions of the Guides and the Developmental Characteristics Chart are also available on the accompanying CD-ROM.

# Acknowledgments

We acknowledge the Alvin H. Einbender Philanthropic Fund and Hilliard and Gloria Farber for liberal financial support from 1993 through 1996. A generous 3-year grant (2000–2003) from the W.K. Kellogg Foundation funded the Visit Training and Dissemination Project and the Visit's Advisory Board. The Project was coordinated and strengthened by Susan Recchia, faculty member at Teachers College, Columbia University. Marvin McKinney of the W.K. Kellogg Foundation provided invaluable insight and support. We conducted numerous rewrites in response to evaluations yielded by two training sessions for key supervisory personnel working with families in a variety of service systems nationwide and in response to the perspective and enthusiastic support of the Visit's Advisory Board members.

We especially thank Emily Fenichel and other members of the staff and board of ZERO TO THREE: National Center for Infants, Toddlers and Families for their unstinting colleagueship and creative advice through the years. In 1983, Rebecca Shahmoon Shanok focused our attention on the observation of parent–child interactions. Tammy Mann helped us emphasize aspects of the Visit that are needed in the field today. Martha Leonard and Sally Provence of the Yale Child Study Center helped us get started. We have tried to allow the spirit of Sally Provence to come alive in the Visit.

We thank invaluable members of the Visit team: Rebecca Bulotsky, Gloria Farber, Loretta Murin, Shawn Plotkin, Hilary Rosa, Yumiko Sekino, and Andronika Tsamas. Siri Carpenter provided essential consulting and editorial services. We thank Dan Polin for the production of videotapes and Gina Lee for her diligence in word processing. We especially thank Jessica Allan, Acquisitions Editor at Paul H. Brookes Publishing Co., for taking our point of view and giving us such clear and useful advice.

Finally, last but not at all least, we thank our husbands, daughters, and grandchildren, who have supported us personally and professionally in many, many ways.

To the babies, toddlers, and parents
who have taught us
and to the guiding spirit of Sally Provence

# 1

# INTRODUCTION TO THE VISIT

The Visit outlines a process that uncovers potential in children, parents, and practitioners. It provides in-service training for direct care practitioners and fosters change in how service systems view and work with babies, toddlers, and their families. The Visit is woven into the ongoing life of the service system. Direct observation, reflection, and synthesis guide the direct care practitioner and his or her supervisor, who work together as a team. The team follows carefully structured protocols for children 2–36 months of age and develops a coherent picture of the child as an individual within the context of his or her family and social-cultural community.

Implementation of the Visit begins with a meeting of the child, the child's parent, the practitioner who works directly with the family, and the practitioner's supervisor. They meet in a home, clinic, or group care setting. Throughout the meeting, the team observes the child's interactions with the parent, self-initiated behavior, and performance on developmental tasks. In keeping with the roles of the supervisor and the direct care practitioner within the service system (see the Glossary for key terms), the supervisor interviews the parent about the child's history, elicits issues of concern, and solicits caregiving advice. Therefore, the direct care practitioner has an opportunity, if the situation allows, to be with the child.

No notes are taken during the meeting. This allows the team and family to focus on one another.

Immediately following the meeting, the direct care practitioner and supervisor review what they have learned from the family. They reflect on their direct observations of the child's behavior and on parent–child interactions. They synthesize their observations with the parent's responses during the reflective parent interview. This synthesis yields a picture of the child in the context of his or her family. The team members discuss their findings and write a letter to the parent. They illustrate the letter with their observations, acknowledge the parent's critical role as the child's primary caregiver, and summarize plans agreed on with the parent for the child's care.

The Visit's findings are not definitive—nor should they be, given the plasticity of development in very young children. As a process of discovery, implementing the Visit can help service providers gain parents' trust and support parents' willingness to work with the service system. The following words by one parent underscore the essential nature of the Visit as an investigation that supports a continuing relationship between family and service system: "When I hear the word 'discover,' sunshine pops into my mind. But 'assessment' and 'evaluation'—you think of piles of paper and raised eyebrows. That's not the purpose. It's to get good things for our child" (Gillies, as cited in Berman & Shaw, 1996, p. 368).

Participation in the Visit with the family and the supervisor enhances the direct care practitioner's observational skills and understanding of the child's developmental strengths and challenges, enabling him or her to provide the best possible care. Through a series of visits, meetings with families, and co-reviews with the supervisor, the direct care practitioner gains a more professional footing and heightens his or her investment in the service system.

Implementation of the Visit benefits the service system by using the nonlinear dynamic systems perspective on development to better understand the child's strengths and challenges as observed in self-initiated behavior and performance of competency tasks. Parental strengths become apparent as the parent interacts with the child, shares concerns, and participates in plans for the child's care. The Visit uncovers these strengths and challenges and thereby can cut costs to the service system sooner rather than later by involving the parent more directly in the child's therapy, finding a more specific intervention, or arranging a diagnostic evaluation with the parent that may secure special services for the child. In addition, the supervisor benefits by gaining firsthand knowledge of the families and direct care practitioners under his or her care. The supervisor discovers what support families and practitioners need—knowledge that he or she can use immediately on site—that is, consultation among the parent, direct care practitioner, and supervisor to suggest special services.

Each visit during the family's participation in the service system offers a situation animated with the hope implicit in every baby and toddler—a situation filled with information that can enrich the lives of the parent, the child, and the practitioners who work with them.

# 2

## THE VISIT IN PRACTICE

This section depicts the Visit in practice through the story of a single mother and her 5-month-old son, Hugo, who were living in a resident shelter for homeless mothers and their children. This example illustrates the power of the Visit to inform a service system by illuminating the strengths of a mother and her baby—in particular, a baby who has an undiagnosed physical delay. Portions of the Visit are described to illustrate what a direct care practitioner and supervisor may uncover through observation, reflection, and synthesis.

### CONDUCTING THE VISIT WITH HUGO

Hugo will attend a child care center while his mother, Violet, participates in a drug treatment program. The Visit is conducted in the shelter's infant/toddler child care room at the shelter one day before Hugo is to begin receiving services. The homeless shelter's director arranged administration of the Visit because she believes that homeless mothers are so focused on survival that caring for their children can become a secondary concern. As for the participation of Hugo's direct care practitioner in the Visit process, the director of the homeless shelter noted that ongoing professional development benefits children receiving services. Hugo's direct care practitioner, Nancy, has a high school diploma and very little training in infant development and practice.

#### MEETING

The direct care practitioner and her supervisor (Jane, the head teacher for the shelter's infant/toddler room) are waiting in the infant/toddler room when Violet enters, carrying Hugo in her arms. The supervisor voices her observation *in the moment*: "Hugo is clinging to you while he tries to understand us. He certainly knows who his Mommy

3

is." Violet smiles and says, "We're buddies." Jane asks Violet to decide how the Visit will begin; she can choose between the tasks for Hugo and the reflective parent interview. Violet demurs. The supervisor says, "You choose. You're in charge here." Violet chooses to give Hugo the tasks first and then engage in the interview.

Hugo's responses to the tasks vary greatly. When Jane pulls him to sit, Hugo's head lags almost painfully, and he does not help the supervisor on the second try. However, the observation of another competency task demonstrates this mother's relationship with her son.

*Hugo lies on his back on the floor. His mother has been asked to sit behind him. Hugo waves his arms and legs gently in the air. The supervisor asks Violet to ring a bell. She rings it lightly two times. Hugo stops waving his arms and legs, and as he stills completely, Violet lets out a soft gasp of amazement. She nods and says, "Yes, he heard it." Then Jane asks Violet to call Hugo's name. When Violet does this, Hugo immediately turns his entire body around so that he can see his mother. She extends her arms toward him as he looks at her and almost rolls over, straining his entire body around and toward her.*

Next, Violet and Jane sit in rocking chairs, facing one another for the reflective parent interview. Violet has placed Hugo on his tummy on a blanket on the floor. Jane asks Nancy to sit beside him, "to be on his level." Nancy secures a few toys and sits down next to Hugo. After a long and comfortable pause, Violet begins to tell their story. She says that she had been on drugs through 7 months of her pregnancy. When asked about Hugo's special needs, Violet says she is very concerned about the tremors Hugo exhibits, especially during sleep. Violet believes that no one in the shelter is interested in the tremors, although they concern her greatly. When asked how she responds to these tremors, Violet tells Jane that she lifts Hugo up and holds him tightly against her chest so he knows that someone is there for him. Violet also wonders about Hugo's eyes because he rubs them a great deal.

The team members thank Violet for sharing with them. They tell Violet they will write her a letter summarizing the meeting.

## CO-REVIEW

The co-review is led by questions posed by the supervisor to the direct care practitioner. As the supervisor and direct care practitioner in this case remember and restate what they learned during their meeting with the family, they synthesize the information provided during the reflective interview with their direct observations evidencing a strong attachment between Hugo and Violet. Hugo's overall use of his motor system was cause for concern, demonstrated by his marked head lag in the pull-to-sit task. In contrast, a task with red rings had revealed Hugo's ability to coordinate his visual and motor systems and, perhaps most important, to remember—hence, his cognitive strength. For instance, the team observed while Jane extended some small red rings toward Hugo's left hand as he lay on his back. When the rings touched his hand, Hugo grasped and held on to them. Jane guided his hand and the rings to his mouth. Then, Hugo shook the rings and brought them back to his mouth independently.

Thus, the team's nonjudgmental observations indicated a lack of coordination among Hugo's social, emotional, cognitive, and motor systems. When compared with other children in his age range, as noted on the Developmental Characteristics Chart (available in this book), Hugo demonstrated severe motor developmental delay. His interactions with his mother and with the team indicated that his social, emotional, and cognitive systems were functioning well, and although his motor behavior was slow, it did improve in the context of social interactions (i.e., when his mother called his name).

## PARENT LETTER

The parent letter grew out of the team members' synthesized picture of the child and his parent. The letter reported Hugo's social and emotional competencies and was illustrated with observations of interactions between Hugo and his mother as well as between Hugo, the supervisor, and the direct care practitioner. The letter emphasized Violet's loving contribution to Hugo's development. It suggested that Violet and Nancy, as Hugo's direct caregivers, encourage Hugo's motor development daily. The letter reassured Violet that Hugo's direct care and other practitioners would observe vigilantly for tremors, especially while Hugo slept. Jane and Nancy would work with Violet to understand the significance of these involuntary movements and would discuss seeking a neurological evaluation if all participants deemed it necessary. Jane and Nancy would also observe Hugo when he rubbed his eyes; they would report to Violet what happened while and just before he did this.

The letter was guided by the team's strong insight that Violet truly cared for Hugo. She was a perceptive advocate for ways to help him develop as fully as possible.

Portions of the letter written for Violet follow:

*Hugo is developing well with regard to his ability to think and solve problems. For example, as he coordinated his eyes and head to follow the ball, he seemed to ask, "Where is it going?" . . . He talks by cooing and moving his entire body. He heard your voice as you sat behind him and turned his body all the way around to see you. In this and other ways, Hugo demonstrated his strong attachment to you. This tells us he trusts you and is beginning to trust others.*

*As noted, we observed Hugo's physical ability to coordinate his eyes and body. Moving his body and lifting his head seem difficult for him. Suggestions for helping him in this area include dressing him in as few items of clothing as possible, positioning him on his belly on the floor, and encouraging him to move his body as much as possible. Toys or your face should be placed in front of Hugo's eyes when he's lying on his belly so that he has to lift his head to see them and hence work on his head control and trunk control.*

*Nancy will observe when he rubs his eyes; she will also observe him when he sleeps. If a tremor (shaking or startle-like movement) is observed, Nancy will lift Hugo from the crib and hold him securely so that he can feel her body, just as you described to us during the reflective parent interview. As you said, this will help Hugo to know that someone is there for him. We are glad you showed us how you hold him and how you feed him his bottle.*

### PARENT'S RESPONSE

In this situation, the parent's response was secured by the director of the homeless shelter, who was not in the infant/toddler child care room at any time during the visit. The director accompanied Violet as she carried Hugo into the residential section of the shelter. The director reported that when Violet entered the room where she and Hugo stayed with the other families, she burst out, "It was great! I learned so much—it made me want to know more about Hugo, his development!"

### DIRECT CARE PRACTITIONER'S EXPERIENCE

A few days later, Jane obtained Nancy's evaluation of the meeting. The supervisor said, "Let's reflect on your experience during Hugo's visit. Did you learn anything special about Hugo and his mother and about infant development, in general?" Nancy replied,

*I learned a lot by watching you. I learned how to observe how Hugo was supposed to be and how he actually was. I found out more about his prenatal development that helped us understand him. The practitioner team was on target as to his developmental delay. He stayed the same. Unfortunately, we did not get to refer him for further evaluation by a neurological pediatrician before he left the shelter. I used my copy of the letter we wrote for his mother with the entire staff.*

Evidently, the direct care practitioner had made herself fully available to learn during the meeting with Hugo and Violet and during the co-review that immediately followed. Nancy began to see Violet as someone she needed to listen to and work with in caring for Hugo and to realize the value of careful observation. As Nancy worked with other children and parents on a daily basis, perhaps she began to synthesize her observations of parent–child interactions and her observations of the child's response to everyday tasks with what she knew of the child's history. Certainly, she was better prepared for conferences with her supervisor, for staff meetings, and for subsequent implementations of the Visit with other families. Nancy's sense of herself as a professional is evident in her evaluation of her experience with her supervisor, Hugo, and Violet. She seemed confident and pleased about presenting Hugo's case in a staff meeting, illustrating her findings with a copy of the letter she and her supervisor had written for Hugo's mother.

## HOW THE VISIT IS INTEGRAL TO THE SERVICE SYSTEM

Gradel, Thompson, and Sheehan (1981) presented research demonstrating that parent reports can be reliable, and Anastasiow and Harel (1993) stressed the value of identifying behaviors that suggest a baby is at early developmental risk. Hugo's story is notable because it shows how conducting the Visit can uncover a parent's and a child's strengths as well as identify behaviors that suggest early developmental risk. Use of the Visit can set in motion timely and cost-effective efforts by a direct care practitioner and supervisor who work together within the same program. As a team, they are capable of activating the larger interrelated service systems. Thus, the Visit provides crucial training for direct care practitioners, changes how service systems view and work with families, and promotes the informed relationships that are basic to efficient practice.

# 3

# Theory and Principles that Guide the Visit

The Visit is grounded in the nonlinear dynamic systems theory and in principles distilled from current knowledge about human growth and development in the earliest years. The nonlinear dynamic systems perspective asks one to observe *how* a child coordinates his or her systems (social-emotional, visual, motor, cognitive, and communication) in order to solve a developmental task in the context of his or her family and larger caregiving system. This perspective de-emphasizes *when* an ability emerges (i.e., at which age). The child is not observed in isolation but as an individual within the larger caregiving system (Sander, 2000). The supervisor's and direct care practitioner's observations are directed toward the child's strengths and the strengths in the parent–child relationship, as illustrated in the following example.

*Five-month-old Byron is sitting on his mother's lap as she, the direct care practitioner, and the supervisor sit on the floor next to a toddler-size table. The supervisor presents a reaching and grasping task by placing a small red cube on the table, in front of Byron and within reachable distance. Byron's hands remain tightly fisted as he lifts his head and attempts to look at the cube. His mother immediately realizes Byron's difficulty and readily adjusts his position on her lap so that he can see the cube more easily. Although Byron does not reach for the cube, his left hand partially opens and moves slightly toward the cube as he looks at it with great curiosity.*

*Later, during the reflective parent interview, Byron sits on his mother's lap. At one point, she begins to gently stroke his tightly fisted right hand. As she does so, Byron's hand opens and he curls his fingers around one of hers.*

Byron initially did not use his motor system to grasp and explore the cube. However, Byron's mother was attuned to him and realized that his position needed adjustment so he could better see the cube. Byron's use of his visual system, one of his strengths, led him to reach toward the cube with his left hand.

The supervisor's use of the nonlinear dynamic systems perspective enabled her to observe the strength in the parent–child relationship, as demonstrated through the mother's attunement to her son. She helped Byron coordinate his vision (visual system) with his reaching and grasping motions (motor system).

As illustrated in this example, the nonlinear dynamic systems perspective helps individuals conducting the Visit to organize and synthesize their observations throughout the Visit, and it provides a theoretical framework for the Visit's four guiding principles:

1. The child is a complex, dynamic system who perceives and simultaneously initiates his or her actions within the environment.
2. The child develops within the context of the family.
3. The parent is the child's primary caregiver.
4. The child's family belongs to one or more social-cultural communities.

## THE CHILD IS A COMPLEX, DYNAMIC SYSTEM

The nonlinear dynamic systems perspective asks the team to observe and analyze how the child coordinates his or her social-emotional, visual, motor, cognitive, and communication systems. Taking this perspective to development enables the team to recognize that the child's competencies are not fixed but, rather, are fluid and adaptable (Sanders, 2000; Thelen, 1989). The team focuses on the child's responses to tasks designed for his or her age range and on the child's self-initiated behavior.

The tasks have two functions: 1) they provide a context for applying the nonlinear dynamic systems perspective to observation, and 2) the tasks help observers analyze how the child uses his or her various systems when solving a task in the context of the parent–child relationship. The tasks are adapted from several standardized and nonstandardized instruments and are coordinated with the Developmental Characteristics Chart listings for the appropriate age range. The team can then use the Developmental Characteristics Chart to measure the child's performance against the performance of other children in the same age range, using age as an externally imposed marker. Using this traditional approach for all children (regardless of prematurity or birth abnormalities) with the nonlinear dynamic systems perspective to development links the Visit with other more traditional instruments. The Visit's findings, in turn, may orient the supervisor and direct care practitioner to speak with the parent about the child's possible need for special services.

Most traditional tools separately examine behavior within each individual domain or system (social-emotional, visual, motor, cognitive, and communication) and are based on the assumption that development progresses in a linear fashion. In contrast, guidance by the nonlinear dynamic systems perspective not only deepens the team's understanding of the child but also emphasizes the fact that development evolves at least in part through the interaction of multiple systems within the child. The non-linear dynamic systems perspective directs observation toward the interplay of these systems. This interplay, influenced by the parent–child relationship, reveals a child's "hidden" strengths, which can be captured by observing the child's external behavior.

The Visit allows practitioners to observe the child as he or she simultaneously perceives the environment and initiates actions—for example, smiling, reaching, or walking. These behaviors, which demonstrate the child's social, cognitive, visual, and motor skills, depend on the child's ability to orchestrate the skills within the context of the parent–child relationship. Therefore, the Visit is grounded in the team's observations of the child's behavior and interactions with his or her parent. The direct care practitioner and supervisor reflect on and synthesize these observations during the co-review. The co-review process allows the team to develop a comprehensive—albeit brief—picture of the child as a dynamic, whole human being and informs their work with the family. In developing this picture with the direct care practitioner, the supervisor draws on his or her knowledge of early development from the maturational, traditional, and nonlinear dynamic systems perspectives.

The following vignettes illustrate how practical application of the nonlinear dynamic systems theory enables a team to organize its observations and to discover how a child's competencies are embedded in the parent–child relationship. The first vignette focuses on a child's self-initiated behavior.

*Nineteen-month-old Katherine, her parents, the direct care practitioner, and the supervisor are sitting on the floor. Before the supervisor introduces the first competency task, Katherine stands, walks toward a ball, and lifts it from the floor. She walks to her father and gives the ball to him. The mother, the direct care practitioner, and the supervisor turn their attention to the father and daughter as the father takes the ball and gently throws it. Katherine follows the ball, picks it up again, and brings it back to her father. "This is a game we play often," Katherine's father comments with a smile on his face.*

As this example illustrates, the Visit allows for a child's self-initiated activity. In fact, the Visit welcomes such unexpected actions, regardless of the situation, as an opportunity to learn more about the child—and, in many cases, the parent. In the preceding scenario, the supervisor had planned to ask Katherine to kick the ball as one of the tasks designed for Katherine's age range. Katherine, however, immediately took the initiative to use the ball in a way that engaged her in a familiar social interaction with her father. This particular situation evidenced the child's ability to initiate a favorite game by coordinating her social-emotional, communication, visual, and motor systems with her memory (cognitive system).

By observing unplanned events from a nonlinear dynamic systems perspective, the team learns how individual children coordinate their systems and which systems they prefer to use when they are interacting with their parents. During their co-review of the meeting, Katherine's direct care practitioner and the supervisor can reflect on and synthesize their observations of Katherine's unexpected action and of comments made during the reflective parent interview. These observations can be included in their parent letter to illustrate the strength of Katherine's relationship with her parents.

The team in the next vignette observes a child with his parents during two tasks within his age range. The team observes which systems the child selects to solve the tasks and how these choices relate to his interactions with his parents. As the two tasks are drawn from standardized instruments, the team uses the Visit's Developmental Characteristics Chart to compare the child's performance with that of other children in the same age range.

*Nine-month-old Billy, his father, the direct care practitioner, and the supervisor are sitting on the floor next to a toddler-size chair and table. Billy's mother sits on the opposite side of the table. The first task is pull to stand. The Visit supervisor asks Billy's mother to place a string of pop beads on the table. Billy's mother wiggles the string of beads gently so that it hangs on the side of the table near Billy. Billy looks at the beads. He shifts his weight in the direction of the beads and reaches for them. However, he can only grasp the string of beads if he pulls himself into a standing position using the chair, which is close to the beads that are hanging over the side of the table. Billy looks toward his father, then scans the environment and shifts his attention to a pillow that is lying on the floor within reachable distance. Billy grasps the pillow with both hands and joyfully bangs it on his legs.*

*Next is the object constancy task. Billy's parents, the direct care practitioner, and the supervisor are sitting around an adult-size table. Billy sits on his father's lap. The supervisor places a red cube on the table in front of Billy, who has one hand in his mouth and the other hand under the table. He looks toward the cube but makes no perceptible move toward it. The supervisor hides the cube under a blue cloth. Billy grasps the cloth and explores it with his eyes and with his mouth. He ignores the cube. It seems that he does not remember the cube hidden under the cloth.*

*The supervisor then asks the direct care practitioner to hide her face with a scarf—that is, to play Peekaboo with Billy. Billy watches her attentively and smiles when she removes the scarf and uncovers her face. Then, Billy's mother plays Peekaboo at the supervisor's suggestion. As she covers her face, Billy vocalizes joyfully, pulls the scarf off of her face, looks at her face, and continues to vocalize as he and his mother play the game.*

In the preceding vignette, Billy chose not to pull himself into a standing position during the pull-to-stand task. Instead of drawing on his motor system, he used his social-emotional system to make eye contact with his father and his visual system to scan the environment and grasp a pillow that was in reachable distance on the floor.

When the red cube was shown to Billy during the object constancy task, he did no more than look at the cube—he did not try to secure it in any way. When the cube was covered, Billy seemed to focus on the blue cloth; then, he grabbed it (motor system) and explored it with his eyes and mouth (visual and oral systems). It is important to note that he appeared to completely ignore the red cube. By taking the nonlinear dynamic systems perspective, the team validated its observations that Billy is well attached to his parents (social-emotional system) and curious, despite his seeming inability to pull to stand (motor system) and to remember a nearby object hidden under a cloth (cognitive system).

In a Peekaboo game, human beings can be seen as objects. In the vignette, Billy gave ample indication that he remembered the object—that is, the direct care practitioner's hidden face. Moreover, Billy vocalized during the game with his mother. The nonlinear dynamic systems perspective directs observation toward the fact that Billy's social-emotional system may be calling forth and strengthening both his ability to remember (cognitive system) and his emerging ability to communicate vocally (communication system).

During the co-review of their exchange with the family, the direct care practitioner and the supervisor shared their observations of Billy's performance of the two tasks. They used the Developmental Characteristics Chart to compare Billy's performance with the performance of other children in his age range. They remember that he did not pull to stand and that he did not seem to remember that the cube was hidden under the cloth. During the Peekaboo game, however, Billy seemed to understand that objects or persons exist even if they cannot be seen. The team agreed to further observe Billy's ability to initiate transitions from one position to another, as this skill related to his motor development. Because it has been demonstrated that early vocalizations and the emergence of words are interrelated (Fogel & Thelen, 1987), the team also agreed to observe Billy's vocalizations and the emergence of words. The team's letter to Billy's parents focused on observations of his strengths with suggestions as to how the team, along with the parents, could encourage Billy's communication and motor development.

Each day, there is always more to learn about young children and their families. Recognition that a child is a complex, dynamic system reinforces how the Visit is an investigation—a process of discovery. The Visit is designed to uncover developmental potential so that the child may grow and develop as a full and active participant within the context of his or her family and the community at large.

## THE CHILD DEVELOPS WITHIN THE CONTEXT OF THE FAMILY

The child brings the parent and practitioners together and is considered an equal and active participant who leads throughout the Visit (Bulotsky, 1995). The child's behavior occurs in this larger caregiving system and provides common ground on which the parent and practitioners can meet; although the parent and practitioners may differ ethnically, socially, or culturally, they connect as they look at, listen to, and discuss the child. The following vignette exemplifies this point.

*Six-month-old Oliver, his parents, the direct care practitioner, and the supervisor are sitting on the floor. Oliver is placed on his tummy; pulling up onto his hands and knees, he rocks back and forth in place. As his mother says, "I feel sorry for him—he sees objects in front of him and pushes back," Oliver pulls himself onto his knees, balances on his hands and knees, and moves his body forward slightly. Then he squeals and again moves forward slightly. Oliver's mother exclaims, "This is the first time he's done that! Maybe that's why he was up so often last night." Oliver continues to squeal and pull up on his hands and knees, moving forward three times. His father applauds and says, "Oliver, you are so big!" The direct care practitioner smiles broadly as the supervisor says, "We have a lot to look forward to in caring for Oliver."*

In this example, the adults experience joy and awe in observing a young human being. While sitting on the floor next to Oliver, the parents and team, each in their own way, explore the baby's point of view. Call (1995) emphasized the value of taking the baby's point of view by urging parents to "ask not only what you can do for your baby but try to be receptive to what your baby can do for you."

The nonlinear dynamic systems theory of development supports the principle that a child is best understood within the context of his or her family system. Therefore, the team is directed to gather fruitful knowledge about the child, both directly and indirectly, during the meeting with the family. During the reflective parent interview, the supervisor obtains information directly from the parent. Meanwhile, the child and the direct care practitioner have an opportunity to begin their relationship by playing together in another part of the room. In this way, the direct care practitioner learns directly from and about the child. In addition to these direct sources of information, the team obtains indirect information about the child in the context of the family system when it observes how the parent and child interact with each other during the meeting. In the co-review, the direct care practitioner and supervisor reflect on their memory of these interactions and integrate them with other information to develop a picture of the child within the family, which they share in their letter to the parent.

## THE PARENT IS THE CHILD'S PRIMARY CAREGIVER

In several public speaking engagements, Urie Bronfenbrenner emphasized the central role of the parent by saying, "The parent is most apt to be crazy about the kid." The Visit is designed to ensure that the parent, who is an inherently powerful influence in the child's life, will be sought out rather than excluded throughout the family's participation in the service system. The Visit offers the team a series of opportunities to reaffirm the parent as the child's primary caregiver—that is, the person who provides the context wherein the child may develop to his or her potential and contribute to the family and community.

Given this understanding, the team seeks specific caregiving details and advice for particular interventions from the parent during the interview. In addition, the team asks the parent to administer specific developmental tasks (e.g., see the special tasks for the parent in the Guide for 10–13 months). Participation in special tasks can mitigate a parent's discomfort with the tasks while allowing the team to observe parent–child interactions, as shown in the following example.

*Maya, 13 months old, has been in a group child care program for 8 months when she, her mother, and the team meet to conduct the Visit. Before the Visit, the direct care practitioner had told the supervisor that the child cries whenever she (the direct care practitioner) leaves the room. During the co-review, however, the direct care practitioner exclaims, "I never thought of Maya's relationship with her mother before—they are so alike!"*

In observing the mother and child together, the direct care practitioner began to recognize the strength of the child's attachment to her mother and the ways in which the two were similar. In this instance, the direct care practitioner's observation of the parent–child interaction opened the way for the supervisor to emphasize the caregiver role. It is the direct care practitioner's job to support and strengthen the family as the primary context within which the child develops.

In other cases, as emphasized by the pediatrician Arthur Parmelee as early as 1989, parents may be concerned about a natural change in a healthy infant's or toddler's behavior, which may require changes in the family environment. Also, in 1981 T.B. Brazelton described such new situations as opportunities, wherein the parent's relationship with the child may be strengthened.

During the co-review process, the team again acknowledges the parent as the child's primary caregiver. The parent's ultimate responsibility as the child's primary caregiver often becomes clear as the team integrates its observations of the child's self-initiated behavior, the child's performance on the tasks, the parent–child interactions, the parent's caregiving advice, and the parent's responses to the interview questions.

Finally, in the follow-up letter to the parent, the supervisor and direct care practitioner share their observations of the parent's beneficial care of the child and summarize mutual understandings reached with the parent during the meeting, further validating the parent's central role in the child's life. Moreover, because the parent receives a letter every time the Visit is conducted, the letters serve as Visit records. Copies of these letters are kept on file within the service system, so information about the child and parent is available to all providers as long as the family participates in the service system.

## THE CHILD'S FAMILY BELONGS TO A SOCIAL-CULTURAL COMMUNITY

A family may belong to a community whose language and culture are unfamiliar to the majority of staff in the service system. As discussed, these differences can be indirectly mediated by the nonverbal communication of the baby or toddler.

The child becomes the mediator and places all Visit participants on common ground, wherein trust and respect can grow to the benefit of the family and the service system. Furthermore, the Visit provides time for the family, the direct care practitioner, and the supervisor to recognize and explore the complex interactions of their individual cultures. The Visit acts on Emde's assertion that "parent, child and provider team will need to set boundaries and limits to what is shared, and there are unique experiences for those in . . . other-oriented (dissimilar) cultures" (1994, p. 730).

In addition, because the Visit is conducted by a team of two practitioners, one may speak the family's language or be familiar with its cultural expectations. Such cultural representation on the team also would inform the co-review process, when the direct care practitioner and supervisor reflect on and synthesize their observations. Each may be able to contribute insights gained through experience within the family's social-cultural community, producing a deeper understanding of the child and family. In particular, when the direct care practitioner's expertise is acknowledged in this way, he or she can feel further empowered as a full member of the team.

If the family cannot read English and one team member is proficient in the family's language, he or she may be able to translate the parent letter either orally or in writing. If neither team member speaks the family's language, a translator can be secured to assist throughout the Visit. It is important that the translator be instructed only to translate, not to give opinions, to secure accurate communication.

The Visit is easily integrated into service systems of various cultural backgrounds, as shown by the following portions of a letter sent to one family. The letter was written after a meeting in which all participants—the supervisor, the direct care practitioner, 5-month-old Aliyha, and Aliyha's grandmother—were Native American. (Aliyha's grandmother was the primary caregiver because Aliyha's parents could not care for her at that time.) In this situation, the Visit took place in their community health and human services system.

*We really enjoyed sharing the Visit with you and Aliyha. We learned a great deal about how culture plays an important role in your lives. It was very good to see how important the relationship is between grandmother and granddaughter.*

*When the Visit first began, Aliyha made direct eye contact with you; she did this several other times throughout the Visit. We observed Aliyha vocalizing and talking to us, even saying "Da Da" and "Ma Ma." You spoke to each other throughout the meeting. You gave Aliyha kisses, pats, and hugs and stroked her hair, which you said she likes very much. Aliyha demonstrated her ability through the tasks, while you supported her by allowing her to show us what she can do.*

*In performing the tasks, Aliyha demonstrated her motor development by grasping the red rings and following them with her eyes, palming the two cubes in both hands, and bringing the crackers to her mouth.*

*We observed your knowledge of your granddaughter's needs when you told us that she likes her hair stroked, that she likes to roll onto her left side, and that you talked to her more than she is used to at home.*

*You expressed to us a concern about Aliyha's educational needs with regard to her Native American culture. We would be happy to assist you in scheduling any appointments at school and will be available to attend these appointments with you if you would like.*

*We also understand the importance of heritage and supporting Aliyha's growth and development through Native American beliefs and practices. We are committed to promoting and protecting your family's rights under the Indian Child Welfare Act.*

*Sharing the Visit was fun and informative. Thank you for spending time with us and allowing us to observe Aliyha's developmental strengths. We are looking forward to learning more about Aliyha and continuing to work with you to support her development within our Native American community.*

This example demonstrates how the Visit strengthens a family by reaffirming culture. The letter in particular was used to recognize the heritage of a culture and to reassure the family that the child would receive care in an environment that supports her family's cultural beliefs and practices.

# 4

## IN-SERVICE TRAINING FOR
## THE DIRECT CARE PRACTITIONER

The Visit provides in-service training for direct care practitioners—training that is integrated into the ongoing life of the service system. The Visit can be conducted any time during the family's participation or immediately after the family enrolls in a service system. Because the system may provide early intervention or perhaps child care for working families, the direct care practitioner may be a social services coordinator, home visitor, caregiver, family child care provider, paraprofessional, or teacher.

### PROFESSIONAL IDENTITY

Training for the Visit may be more aptly termed *experience* because it is provided during a series of visits with one or more families. Such experience reinforces the direct care practitioner's sense of him- or herself as a professional whose job offers many opportunities to enhance the well-being of children and families. This reinforcement happens quite naturally as the direct care practitioner and the supervisor work as a team throughout the Visit process. During the meeting with the family, the direct care practitioner's importance is reaffirmed by his or her presence (signifying full participation in the Visit) and by the supervisor's acknowledgment that the direct care practitioner is the person who works most often with the child. During the co-review that immediately follows the meeting, the supervisor questions the direct care practitioner. The direct care practitioner's answers guide the co-review, revealing how and what he or she observed during the meeting with the family. The supervisor respects these answers and any silences, relating them to previous comments shared by the direct care practitioner. If the direct care practitioner's observations are clouded by personal judgment of a child and/or a parent's behavior, the supervisor has an opportunity to stress what can be learned by reflecting on an observation before making a judgment. In addition, throughout the co-review the supervisor is able to relate current knowledge about early child development to what the team experienced during the meeting with the family. Thus, he or she is able to engage in reflective supervision about what the team jointly experienced with the family (this can be done regarding the initial meeting and follow-ups). As Emily Fenichel described,

> Reflection in the course of supervision and mentorship helps the trainee come to terms with what it means to go beyond doing what "comes naturally" to help babies or parents—to become a professional who works with infants, toddlers, and their families. Part of the process of developing a professional identity involves recognizing the need to enlarge one's own knowledge, skills, and sensitivity. (1992, p. 13)

Moreover, the direct care practitioner or the supervisor may be from the same culture as the family. One of them may be familiar with the family's cultural expectations. Thus, during the co-review, the team may exchange insights gained through their experiences within the family's social-cultural community. This exchange produces a deeper understanding by the team of a parent's behaviors or comments. A direct care practitioner who is encouraged to share his or her cultural knowledge in this way begins to realize his or her special ability to contribute to the team's understanding of the family.

For example, during one co-review, the team was discussing a mother's attempts to push her 4-month-old child's arm toward a red cube (the task focused on the child's ability to grasp the red cube). The direct care practitioner said that she, like the child's family, was from Puerto Rico. The direct care practitioner suggested that the mother's eagerness for her little boy to successfully perform each task might reflect the family's cultural background. In their shared culture, love is sometimes expressed by the expectation of success.

In addition, team aspects of the Visit deepen the direct care practitioner's awareness of him- or herself as a professional. For instance, the direct care practitioner's participation in the meeting and co-review, guided by reflective supervision, is considered essential. This sense of full participation is capped off with the letter to the parent, which the direct care practitioner and supervisor draft and sign as a team.

Overall, the Visit fulfills, in large part, the four elements of training identified by Eggbeer, Mann, and Gilkerson (2003, p. 35):

1. Opportunities for developing and understanding the importance of observation;
2. Individualized reflective supervision;
3. Collegial support; and,
4. A core knowledge base gained through these three elements.

These four items strengthen the direct care practitioner's professional identity.

## ENHANCED SKILLS IN OBSERVING
## THE PARENT–CHILD RELATIONSHIP

Participating in a series of visits with a supervisor strengthens the direct care practitioner's ability first to observe, then to uncover the meaning of the observation, and finally to intervene according to what he or she has learned from a child's behavior or a parent–child interaction. The direct care practitioner's observational ability will become increasingly evident in his or her work with the children and families served.

Why the emphasis on observation? D.W. Winnicott (1986) emphasized the importance of direct observation of parent–child interactions. He argued that the child's sense of self depends on how the parent responds to the child's innate potential as expressed through spontaneous gestures. At the Center for Infants and Parents, we observed that as the parent and child interact over time, they build a repertoire of interactions, which reflects their individual style as a dyad and the quality of their relationship with one another. As Emde noted, both child behaviors of concern and those that signal optimal development can be "more characteristic of the [parent–child] relationship than the individual" child (1994, p. 7). According to Stanley Greenspan,

> It is in the context of relationships with important caregivers that babies and toddlers develop—and demonstrate—their cognitive, motor, and language skills, as well as intentionality and motivation. Spontaneous interactions between young children and their familiar caregivers reveal core functional interactive capacities. These capacities are the glue that holds the child's development together. (1996, p. 232)

Thus, prior to the Visit's family meetings, the supervisor instructs the direct care practitioner to observe how the parent and child interact with one another. When the Visit was conducted with 14-month-old Joseph and his family, for instance, the supervisor suggested that the direct care practitioner leave the sofa and join Joseph, his mother, and the supervisor on the floor. Both Joseph and his mother had spina bifida. The direct care practitioner, who was a social services coordinator working in an intervention system for babies and toddlers with disabilities, reported that the opportunity to observe Joseph and his mother in this way helped the direct care practitioner (in this case, the social services coordinator) fulfill her goals in working with the family:

*The Visit was absolutely beneficial and useful for my work with the family. . . . I realized how important it was to actually pay attention to what the child was doing. By observing him during the Visit, we realized how he compensated for his mother's inability to engage with him visually. . . . I got to see how eager Joseph was to spend time with his mom, and I had never been with them on the floor nor seen them on the floor together.*

During the team's co-review of the meeting with Joseph's family, the supervisor commented on this direct care practitioner's ability to observe the parent–child interactions in a nonjudgmental manner. An observation is more apt to be clouded with judgment if made from the sofa rather than from the floor at the child's eye level. The direct care practitioner might have simply described the mother and child's disabilities, in which case the team would have been unable to use the direct care practitioner's observation to better understand the family and subsequently plan services.

What if the direct care practitioner's observation is judgmental? The supervisor can encourage the direct care practitioner to step back and describe what happened in concrete words—that is, a description of events as if it were happening again before the team members. This clear image enables the team to uncover the interaction's clues about the strengths and challenges of both the child and the parent in a nonjudgmental way.

In the 1960s, Sally Provence gave a talk in Philadelphia about the power of commenting *in the moment* on a mutually beneficial parent–child interaction. The Visit incorporates this important component, as shown in the following example taken from Joseph's visit.

*The director of an early intervention program suggested that a mother and her son, both of whom have spina bifida, participate in the Visit because the mother seems to be unhappy, to have low self-esteem, and to have little interest in 14-month-old Joseph's care. The Visit is conducted in the family's home and begins with the reflective parent interview, during which Joseph lies on a blanket on the floor. A few toys are placed on the blanket by Joseph's grandfather, who interacts with the child throughout the interview. Joseph's mother sits on the couch. Her eyes are cast downward, averted from Joseph. During the task portion of the Visit, the supervisor asks Joseph's mother to sit on the blanket and rest her back against the couch.*

*The team observes that after Joseph's mother sits on the blanket, Joseph begins to inch toward her on his belly and rests his arm and his head on her leg. She does not glance toward Joseph until the supervisor comments* in the moment *that Joseph is imitating his mother as she pushes her finger through a hole in the blanket. Joseph's mother smiles slightly, glances at Joseph, and playfully imitates him. A game emerges between them. Later, when Joseph's mother is asked how she felt during the family meeting, she says, "I felt happy. Joseph is sociable and likes to play with people."*

Joseph's behavior indicated his wish to be near his mother and to play with her. The supervisor's articulation *in the moment* made this behavior apparent to Joseph's mother—and to the direct care practitioner. In turn, the direct care practitioner will likely be more aware of the power of nonjudgmental direct observations shared *in the moment*. She may share her own direct observations *in the moment* to empower this or another parent with whom she works on a daily basis.

Attachment between parent and child has been carefully researched and described in the literature (Bowlby, 1951; Karen, 1994) and is reflected in parent–child interactions. The interactions—or lack thereof—can occur when the Visit is conducted at home or in a group care setting or simply by chance during a surprise meeting with the family. In group care settings, these interactions are observed most often when the parent and child separate at the beginning of the day or when they reunite at its end.

If the team members are concerned about attachment, they can use the co-review period to share, reflect on, and synthesize their observations of parent–child interactions throughout the Visit meetings. The co-review gives the supervisor an opportunity to relate the meaning of the team's observations not only to the parent's comments during the interview but also to the supervisor's knowledge of child development. In the case of Maya and her mother (see page 15 in Chapter 3), the supervisor was able to impart her knowledge about attachment by relating the child's attempts to be with the direct care practitioner to the child's relationship with her mother. Due to scheduling, the direct care practitioner had never seen Maya and her mother together. The observation, combined with reflection and synthesis by the team, helped the caregiver define her role in the child care situation as secondary to and dependent upon Maya's relationship with her mother. The direct care practitioner's awakened understanding of attachment likely informed her work with not only Maya and her mother but with other children and families in her care.

## INFORMED PRACTICE

Informed practice must be grounded in the direct care practitioner's belief that his or her daily work with families is crucial for the families and the service system. As stated previously, the direct care practitioner becomes aware of this by sharing his or her observations, reflecting on them, and synthesizing them with the supervisor. This process takes place in each visit, helping the direct care practitioner to sharpen his or her observational skills on a daily basis. Children served are able to inform the direct care practitioner about themselves, suggesting interventions timed to their actual behavior. "Teachable moments" emerge, to the benefit of the direct care practitioner and the children. For example, one of two caregivers in the infant room turns from placing a cassette in the tape player and observes that Peter, 8 months old, is up on his knees and reaching toward a set of rings on the child-size table. She walks quickly across the room and moves the rings to the edge of the table. She continues to observe Peter as he pulls himself up on the table and grasps the rings. Thus, Peter demonstrates that he can be somewhat autonomous at 8 months of age.

A direct care practitioner may have attended an off-site lecture or joined an on-line discussion group that stressed the importance of relationships in working with children and families. However, the direct care practitioner must translate this knowledge into his or her own work. During the use of the Visit, the direct care practitioner and his or her supervisor uncover how observation of a child's behavior can be understood as a reflection of relationships within his family. Through this process of mutual discovery with the supervisor, concrete evidence that human relationships are basic to a child's development becomes immediately apparent. Also, the direct care practitioner is apt to share this firsthand experience at off-site workshops or in on-line discussions about relationships between the child and family. He or she will be an informed listener and participant at off-site workshops and staff meetings as well.

A series of visits will enhance and, in turn, inform the direct care practitioner about what can be learned as one relates in an exploratory way with parents, children, and the supervisor. Yet, such knowledge of relationships is not important for the direct care practitioner only: The Visit provides an experience and education, demonstrating the potential empowerment of human relationships for all participants.

## FOLLOW-UP

How do the direct care practitioner and supervisor know if use of the Visit has strengthened the direct care practitioner's daily work with families? The Further Supervision of Direct Care Practitioner Form composes the last portion of the Observation, Reflection, Synthesis Guide and Visit Record for all eight age ranges. The team's experience during a visit, along with the supervisor's notes on the Further Supervision of Direct Care Practitioner Form, may require an immediate follow-up conference. As during the co-review, the follow-up conference is led by the direct care practitioner's answers to nonjudgmental questions posed by the supervisor. The conference usually begins with the supervisor's asking the direct care practitioner to share what participation in the Visit taught him or her and, perhaps, how he or she is using this knowledge in practice on a daily basis. Specific aspects of the direct care practitioner's performance during the Visit that are noted on the Further Supervision of Direct Care Practitioner Form can be woven into the conference. Through a nonjudgmental discussion, the direct care practitioner is led to acknowledge his or her inherent skills and to strengthen the weaker aspects of his or her work.

The follow-up conference is very important, as it provides immediate training feedback and the opportunity for further reflection and insights regarding the direct care practitioner's practice. Information garnered in this manner strengthens the effectiveness of other methods the service system uses to improve service provision by direct care practitioners.

# 5

# ROLE OF THE SUPERVISOR

The supervisor is largely responsible for fulfilling the mission of the Visit: to nurture and inform families and direct care practitioners. The supervisor represents the program or system as a whole—he or she is the person to whom direct care practitioners report and can refer families to discuss a procedure, program policy, or personal concern. The supervisor's rigorous but nonjudgmental observations of the family and of the direct care practitioner guide the meeting during which all participants exchange information. These observations and the personal, professional manner of the supervisor enable him or her to facilitate an atmosphere of trust among all participants, wherein they experience the power of mutual relationship. During the co-review, the supervisor and direct care practitioner work to reflect on and synthesize their observations with the parent's responses during the reflective parent interview. Thus, the supervisor acts as part of a team to garner insights and direction for his or her work with the family.

At the same time, the Visit is beneficial for the supervisor. In observing children and their parents directly, the supervisor obtains a fuller understanding of individual families' needs and how staff can best work with each family. The Visit is a process that should be repeated periodically after enrollment and when deemed necessary by the staff (e.g., when a family signals distress). Thus, the Visit provides the supervisor with many opportunities for observation and reflective supervision, wherein he or she and the direct care practitioner begin to formulate solutions that are individualized for a particular family.

Regardless of the context (e.g., home visit, group child care) during which the Visit occurs, the supervisor needs to remember certain "nuts and bolts," which are detailed in the Guides for each age range and strengthen the Visit and hold it together. In brief, the supervisor prepares by reviewing the "For the Supervisor" section near the beginning of each Guide. He or she speaks with the direct care practitioner immediately before the team meets with the family. The supervisor asks the direct care practitioner to observe parent–child interactions because of their influence on the child's growth and development. Once all participants are present, the supervisor asks the parent to choose whether to begin with the tasks or the reflective parent interview. No notes are taken by the team members during their meeting with the family. As noted previously, the entire meeting is led by the Visit supervisor's observations of the child, the parent, and the direct care practitioner.

The co-review is the supervisor's opportunity for reflective supervision. The co-review is based on the direct care practitioner's answers to questions posed by the supervisor. Reflecting together, they synthesize their observations made throughout the meeting with what the parent shared—about the child and about him- or herself— during the reflective parent interview.

The example that follows illustrates how reflective supervision provides an opportunity for the direct care practitioner of a 4-month-old to uncover a challenge in the parent–child relationship. She was asked to remember if the baby's mother might have interfered with his ability to perform the task with the red rings.

*The supervisor asks the direct care practitioner if she has any questions about how the mother is supporting the baby's development. When the direct care practitioner replies, "No," the supervisor asks if, at any time, the mother indicated possible interference with the baby's ability to grow into an autonomous toddler. The direct care practitioner remembers the mother's response to the ring task: The mother lifted her son's arm toward the rings. The baby kept his fist closed. After the mother sat back and the rings were again presented above the baby's face, the child began to open his fists and brought them both toward the rings. Because of this observation, the practitioner team agreed that they needed to observe for and support this child's initiating gestures and to encourage his mother (verbally and in the parent letter) to do the same at home.*

Later, the team synthesized this observation with information shared by the mother during the reflective parent interview. Learning about the child's difficult birth, which may have given the mother concern for her son's development, helped the team members better understand the mother's attempts to manipulate the child's behavior during the tasks. This synthesis of the reflective parent interview and the team members' observations of interactions between parent and baby helped the team decide how to work with the family and how to write the letter to the baby's mother.

## GUIDED BY DIRECT OBSERVATION

Direct, nonjudgmental observations of the child's behavior and parent–child interactions during the meeting are the foundation for the supervisor's work with the direct care practitioners and the families they serve. For this reason, the supervisor is reminded in the Tasks section of each Guide that he or she must withhold interpretation while observing the child's behavior and the parent–child interactions. The supervisor allows these same observations to guide his or her actions during the meeting while saving his or her uninterpreted observations for the co-review so that joint reflection and interpretation can occur. However, the supervisor is encouraged to comment *in the moment* when he or she observes a child's self-initiated behavior or a parent–child interaction that obviously reflects a parent's supportive caregiving. Commenting *in the moment* reaffirms the parent's role as primary caregiver and demonstrates what both the direct care practitioner and the parent can learn. When these observations are included in the letter to the parent, they reaffirm the child's and the parent's strengths. The supervisor's keen and accurate observation is key to the Visit—both for the family and for the direct care practitioner, who is being alerted to what can be learned through his or her own observations.

The meeting provides three specific and different contexts within which the supervisor and the direct care practitioner can observe interactions between child and parent: tasks for the child, the reflective parent interview, and the child's self-initiated behavior. During the tasks, the supervisor presents the child with a few developmental tasks, which have been carefully selected from a wide range of standardized instruments that practitioners use to compare an individual child's performance to that of other children in the same age range. The child's responses may direct the team to observe further, schedule a conference with the parent, and decide with the parent to make a referral for a third-party screening. Moreover, the nonlinear dynamic systems perspective structures the observations of the team members and allows them to observe which systems the child chooses to perform a task and how the parent and child interact with one another.

The parent is also asked to administer a few everyday tasks—for example, playing Peekaboo or fitting pieces into a puzzle. The supervisor and direct care practitioner observe how the parent presents the tasks. Careful observation can open up a deeper understanding of the relationship between child and parent. An important question to keep in mind is, "How does the parent influence the child's behavior and vice versa?"

The reflective interview with the parent provides another opportunity for the practitioner team to observe parent–child interactions. Before the Visit begins, the supervisor instructs the direct care practitioner not to try to keep the child quiet or away from the parent during the interview. Not only will the interview allow the parent to share the parent's and child's important experiences, it also can be seen as a time of competing with the child for the parent's attention. The parent's reaction may be notable—for example, if the parent does not respond to the cries, calls, or gestures of his or her child while engaged in the reflective parent interview. Perhaps a parent delights in his or her child's performance during the tasks but does not turn toward the child, who may even be crying in the arms of the direct care practitioner. This seemingly contradictory behavior, which evidences the complexity of the parent–child relationship, can lead to a deeper understanding of how best to work with the family.

The reflective parent interview includes questions similar to those found in clinically based interviews. The questions were selected and honed through testing and feedback over the years with parents at the Center for Infants and Parents (Sekino, 1995). Field trials of the Visit validated these questions as being useful and powerful (Axtmann, 2000). The Visit contains few questions, providing ample time for the parent to wait and reflect. After reflecting, the parent is able to share his or her feelings about important experiences such as the child's birth, past separations between child and parent, and intergenerational values. If both parents are present, one may step in and answer for the other, thus revealing certain aspects of their relationship. One interview question asked at the first and subsequent visits—"What are your child's special needs?" (in terms of caregiving)—is particularly important, and the parent is given ample time to answer it. In preparing for the visit, the supervisor determines the order of the questions to ask the parent by referring to what he or she may have learned from a previous visit with the family, from an enrollment form, or from other service providers who have worked with the family.

As shown in the next vignette, direct observations of the child's self-initiated behaviors during the reflective parent interview, and during the tasks, can also afford the supervisor an opportunity to draw the parent's and the direct care practitioner's attention to what can be learned from the child.

*A Chinese mother; her 30-month-old daughter, Yifan; the child's direct care practitioner (a family child care provider); and the direct care practitioner's supervisor (the intervention program's director) initially gathered in the living room of the family child care home. The direct care practitioner had pulled a small table to the middle of the room so Yifan and her mother could work on a puzzle together—a task found in the Observation, Reflection, Synthesis Guide for 30–36 months. Yifan is unable to complete the task despite continual directions from her mother about how to fit the puzzle pieces together.*

*Now it is time for the parent interview: The mother, supervisor, and direct care practitioner (family child care provider) move toward chairs at the kitchen table. At the same time, Yifan pushes the small table back against the wall and aligns two small chairs under it. She does this with vigor and without prompting. At that moment, the supervisor says, "Thank you, Yifan. You must help your mother at home."*

The supervisor drew attention to Yifan's competency and the parent's ability to encourage responsibility in her child. Yifan took this initiative on her own. Her actions, entirely self-initiated, contradicted her inability to complete the puzzle. Later, during the co-review, the practitioner team members had an opportunity to discuss how the contrast of Yifan's inability to complete the puzzle with her mother and her very competent self-initiated behavior might affect their work with the family.

## ESTABLISHING PRIORITIES

One outcome of the Visit should be that the parent, the child, and the direct care practitioner gain from the supervisor a feeling of support that is strengthened by positive expectations for the future, regardless of problems that may occur. This outcome, largely dependent on how the supervisor conducts the visit, takes precedence over the amount—but not the precision—of information gained during the meeting. To accommodate the many demands on practitioners who work with families, the Visit has been honed to approximately 1 hour for both the meeting and the co-review. However, an hour can impose constraints as the supervisor focuses on creating a mutual alliance among the family, direct care practitioner, and him- or herself. Moreover, because the co-review is based on the team members' memories, it must immediately follow the meeting. It may be necessary to make choices about time usage during the course of the team's meeting with the family. The following vignette describes a choice made by one supervisor that yielded an important and useful insight about the ability of one family to focus on their baby's needs while answering questions of importance to them.

*The parent interview is in progress, and the parents have been asked, "How does John tell you he is hungry or tired?" Three-month-old John, who is in the arms of the direct care practitioner, cries and then screams. His mother says, "That's his hunger cry," but neither she nor John's father move toward their baby. After a full minute has passed, during which the screams become louder, the father stands, takes John from the direct care practitioner and gives John to the mother, who then nurses John. Although three questions remain for the parent interview, the supervisor, the direct care practitioner, and the father sit quietly and respectfully for more than 3 minutes, observing the mother and child. When the nursing session comes to a close, the supervisor ends the meeting by saying that the team looks forward to more conversations with the family. The direct care practitioner and supervisor say good-bye to the parents, who smile in anticipation of the same respectful support they have experienced during this first meeting with the team.*

In this vignette, the supervisor decided to leave some interview questions for later. This choice was based on her recognition that creating a mutual alliance with the family was the essential and continuing task.

## A PERSONAL PROFESSIONAL STYLE

How the Visit is conducted will, of course, incorporate the personal professional style of each supervisor. Jeree Pawl (1995) emphasized the importance of being oneself as much as possible when working with families. To ensure valid assessment, the supervisor must follow the Visit's Guides rigorously, yet he or she should do so in a manner that contributes to the establishment of relationships that support the child's well-being.

In an unpublished talk given in New York City on September 26, 1997, Pawl emphasized that how we feel about and behave toward the persons we hope to engage is crucial in forming a potentially positive relationship that allows us to work with them in whatever ways we need to. Acknowledging that the earliest human relationships are wondrous and complex, the supervisor approaches and conducts the Visit as an exploration for him- or herself, the family, and the direct care practitioner who will work most often with the family. The first visit provides an opportunity for the supervisor to initiate a social context to nourish and support the child's developmental potential. Subsequent visits reaffirm and strengthen this context of mutual relationships—a requirement for the child to develop as a full and active participant within his or her family and, eventually, within the community.

In addition to his or her respectful attitude toward the child and family throughout the use of the Visit, the supervisor has many opportunities to demonstrate respect for the direct care practitioner as a professional. For example, this can occur while the supervisor provides reflective supervision by asking questions and allowing the direct care practitioner's answers to guide the co-review. Clarification and amplification in response to the direct care practitioner's answers will emerge as the team members reflect and synthesize what they have learned from the child and parent during the family meeting. In addition, a true in-service training experience with lasting benefit for the direct care practitioner requires the supervisor to begin the Visit with the expectation that he or she will learn and gain new insight from the direct care practitioner, the child, and the parent.

# 6

# BENEFITS TO THE SERVICE SYSTEM

The Visit is a dynamic and primarily nonlinear process of discovery; as such, it embodies Urie Bronfenbrenner's ecological approach to understanding human development in context: "Behavior evolves as a function of the interplay between person and environment" (1979, p. 16). Bronfenbrenner describes this interplay as occurring within many kinds of human systems, with both biological and cultural contexts influencing all participants within the system.

When the child, the parent, and the team come together during the family meeting, they form and strengthen a new social system, becoming a nucleus within the individual program and/or larger service system. For this nucleus to grow, develop, and fulfill its potential, the Visit—with its in-service training component, ability to uncover strengths in the child and family, as well as questions about the child's development—not only must be repeated periodically but also must fit comfortably within whatever service system or program elects to use it.

Field trials of the Visit conducted in a homeless shelter, early intervention programs, and a child care center in a large urban area indicated that the Visit can function easily within a variety of service systems for infants, toddlers, and their families. This outcome can be attributed to the Visit's focus on strengthening human relationships, which requires the supervisor, through direct observation, to adapt the Visit's procedure and materials to the individual child, family, and situation. A colleague who acted as the supervisor during several field trials reported that the requirement to be guided by her observations enabled her to conduct the Visit regardless of the family and situation (Axtmann, 2000).

## INVIGORATES HOW THE SERVICE
## SYSTEM VIEWS AND WORKS WITH FAMILIES

Professionals need a comprehensive view of a family if they are to support and strengthen its well-being. In many service systems, the child's behavior can be questioned by staff. Then, a professional with a specific discipline—for example, a developmental speech therapist or a physical therapist—is asked to observe the child, often without the parent. If the parent is absent, intervention can be based solely on the child and the child's weaknesses. Weaknesses should not be identified without the understanding and consideration of the parent's ability to elicit the child's developmental potential. Because the parent is an active participant during the Visit, insights become available to the supervisor and the direct care practitioner as they discard a possible tendency to judge and stereotype the family. During the co-review, they may get a new view of the family as they carefully consider a number of factors: their individual observations of parent–child interactions; the child's birth and subsequent experiences with intergenerational issues, as elicited during the reflective parent interview; the child's physical health, as reported by the parent (or verified by the parent to be reported on the service system's health form); and, most important, the parent's special concerns about the child's behavior and, perhaps, development.

## UNCOVERS STRENGTHS OF CHILD AND PARENT

The following vignette demonstrates how the Visit can change a service system's view of and work with a family.

*Oscar, who is 18 months old, has been diagnosed with Down syndrome and various medical problems. Because Oscar was exposed to drugs in utero and abandoned by his mother, he was placed by the intervention agency with a foster parent soon after birth. The director of the agency requested a field trial of the Visit. There had been service system difficulties—that is, Oscar often pushes away his many in-home therapists.*

*The Visit takes place in the foster mother's home. The foster mother speaks no English, so the Visit is conducted by a field trial research member who speaks Spanish. Oscar sits on his foster mother's lap during the reflective parent interview. In preparation for the developmental tasks, the foster mother is asked to take off Oscar's socks. She gives one of his socks a slight pull and, speaking softly, guides Oscar's hands to the sock. Oscar pulls off both socks independently. Thus, he demonstrates the emergence of self-help competency, which is being nurtured by his foster mother.*

An important observation from this meeting was the foster mother's expectation that Oscar could do things for himself. She told the field trial team that the various in-home therapists had asked her to leave the room while they were there. This information carried implications of how to work with Oscar and his foster mother. For instance, the supervisor presented Oscar with a wide range of tasks. She did not stereotype Oscar by presenting only tasks below his chronological age; as a result, the supervisor created a nonjudgmental atmosphere of exploration wherein Oscar was able to show his special strengths. Oscar identified himself and his foster mother in a mirror (a 14-month characteristic on the Developmental Characteristics Chart).

During their co-review of the meeting, the direct care practitioner and her supervisor discussed their observations and agreed that Oscar's foster mother was providing a nurturing context, giving Oscar opportunities to develop into an autonomous child. They asked Oscar's foster mother not to leave the room during Oscar's in-home therapy sessions and to help the therapists in their work with Oscar. The social services coordinator was in a position to communicate the foster mother's natural mothering ability to Oscar's therapists.

## REDUCES COSTS

The next example shows how the Visit can reduce costs to the service system by identifying and capitalizing on a parent's strengths.

*A 7-month-old baby who had been exposed to drugs in utero was abandoned by her mother at birth. The child had been placed in foster care and referred for hospital-based physical therapy because of a possible developmental delay. This referral was made in the hospital where the child was born, based on a follow-up assessment process that was routine for children at risk and before placement in a foster home. When the Visit was later conducted with the child's foster family, the direct care practitioner (the child's social services coordinator) and her supervisor observed that the foster mother and baby enjoyed a playful pull-to-sit game. This game had already honed and strengthened the baby's control of her upper body.*

The team's direct observations revealed that the foster mother was exercising the baby's control of her body through the baby's daily care. Thus, the team was able to help the foster mother build on what she was doing naturally. They enlisted her aid in monitoring the baby's motor development. In this instance, conducting the Visit not only supported the child and family but also eliminated the need for hospital-based therapy and therefore cut special services costs. During subsequent visits with the family, the team will have the opportunity to monitor the baby's development with the foster mother and to refer the child for further special services if they observe these are needed.

Staff turnover can disorient everyone in the service system and incur considerable costs. Direct care practitioners may leave because they secure a more lucrative job or finish an educational program that offers different job opportunities. Participation of direct care practitioners in a series of visits with supervisors and families can open up unrealized challenges and points of satisfaction. In field trials of the Visit, various participants, from social services coordinators to child care practitioners, noted practice pointers and leadership opportunities that they gained from participating in the Visit. Recognizing these issues increased their satisfaction with their jobs and influenced them to continue working within their service systems.

## BUILDS TRUST

A truly beneficial caregiving experience for the child requires trust among the parent, the child, and those who care for them. Erik Erikson (1950) showed that trust is the first stage of development for the child and the foundation of adult relationships. The Visit fosters trust among the child, the parent, and the team (Sekino, 1995). The presence of the direct care practitioner and the supervisor at the meeting with the family assures the parent that these two practitioners will work together for the child's well-being. Indeed, the ability of the child and parent to benefit from the program can depend on how much they trust the direct care practitioner and his or her supervisor during the family's participation in the service system.

Building trust can be especially important when a family has just enrolled in a new child care setting. Parents can be apprehensive about daily handing over their baby for care by one or more strangers in a home or group setting. The structure of the Visit helps to dissipate this apprehension. For example, in the reflective parent interview during the family meeting, the supervisor invites the parent to share his or her experiences and feelings as a parent, to express concerns about the child, and to advise the team on ways to care for the child. Asking the parent, "What are your child's special needs?" invites the parent to "own" the child's in- or out-of-home care—to be present (although perhaps not physically) in the child's care. When the Visit is conducted in the home, the direct care practitioner (in this case, perhaps the home visitor) may begin to understand the parent's reluctance to welcome a stranger. In a group care situation, the team can plan to interact with the parent and child in specific ways that will ease the parent's apprehension about leaving the child in the group care setting. The following vignette illustrates how listening to a parent's experience and advice can facilitate the development of trust:

*Aaron is a cheerful 10-month-old who has experienced frequent hospitalizations and was recently enrolled in a group care program. He performs well on the Visit's developmental tasks, yet his parents express fear that the hospitalizations have impeded his development. The supervisor asks the parents for caregiving advice. They tell the team that Aaron quiets down with one of his favorite books and naps in his stroller. The direct care practitioner is careful to read these same books and place Aaron in his stroller at naptime during his first days in group care. Aaron sleeps well, and his parents are less apprehensive because the direct care practitioner trusts and follows their advice. They begin to trust everyone in the program—and Aaron's ability to function there as well.*

Because children may cry or behave in puzzling ways, the reflective parent interview includes questions directly related to separation of the parent and child:

- "Have you and your child been separated?"
- "Who else cared (or cares, if ongoing) for your child?"
- "How did (or do) you feel about it?"

In sharing these experiences and feelings with an interested supervisor, the parent is validated as the child's most important care provider. So validated, it can be easier for the parent to acknowledge his or her own feelings and to implement a process of transition into a more complex kind of care that takes those feelings, as well as the child's feelings, into account.

Trust becomes even more important when the family has special concerns or the child's social-cultural or ethnic background differs from that of the community's majority. The Visit can help the team begin to understand parent–child interactions that the team may find confusing and how these interactions may be a function of the family's cultural style. As we have discussed, it is especially beneficial if one member of the team shares the family's ethnic background and primary language. When this person is the direct care practitioner, he or she is an especially valuable link among the family, other program practitioners, and the supervisor as day-by-day concerns and events emerge.

As discussed in Chapter 5, the order and manner in which the supervisor presents the interview questions emphasize the uniqueness of each family. This dialogue between the parent and supervisor can enhance the parent's belief that the service system is truly sympathetic to the parent and his or her child. In the case of a home visiting program, the parent's or foster parent's apprehension about having strangers in the home usually recedes during the meeting with the team. The parent becomes aware that his or her advice and knowledge are valued and will guide his or her child's care. This increased trust can make the child, the parent, and other family members more available for work with the home visitor or social services coordinator. Moreover, other specialists who are selected by the service system to work with the child in the home may find the family more open to them.

## ALLOWS TIMELY REFERRAL FOR SPECIAL SERVICES

Even when children are enrolled in a service system, their individual needs and those of their families can be overlooked or taken for granted. The Visit can alert the members of a service system to these needs and serve as a link between the programs for children with unidentified needs and the programs and individuals that provide necessary special services. For children who are already receiving a specific intervention, the comprehensive nature of the Visit can clarify and deepen the team's and, hence, the specialist's understanding of the child's strengths, the parent's strengths, and the effect of the parent–child relationship on the child's development. Developing such understanding can help the specialist work with the parent.

Unlike the Diagnostic Classification: 0–3 (Diagnostic Classification of Mental and Developmental Disorders of Infancy and Early Childhood; Weider, 1994), the Visit is not designed to diagnose behaviors that suggest mental health issues or problems in the parent–child relationship. However, the Visit recognizes the basic importance of the child's mental health by requiring the practitioner team to observe parent–child interactions throughout their family meeting and to use the co-review process to integrate these observations with observations of the child's self-initiated behaviors, the child's performance of the tasks, and the parent's answers during the reflective parent interview. If the child's performance on the Visit's tasks suggests developmental concerns, a conference can be arranged with the parent. During the conference, the parent, the direct care practitioner, and the supervisor may agree to secure an Infant-Toddler Developmental Assessment (Provence, Erikson, Vater, & Palermi, 1995) for the family. They may refer the family to a developmental pediatrician, a physical therapist, or a developmental speech therapist and hearing specialist. If the parent agrees, the Visit supervisor may also ask a social worker to visit the home. The following example demonstrates how the Visit led to specialized services for one family.

*Six-month-old Lucas's parents have brought him to his child care center for their first visit. Lucas lies on his belly on the floor mat. As he pushes himself up onto his hands, he emits gurgling sounds, which turn into vigorous squeals. Another squeal cascades forth after the supervisor pulls Lucas up twice from the mat to a sitting position. In both cases, Lucas coordinates his emotional, motor, and vocal systems to his advantage. Later, Lucas is sitting on his father's lap when his mother is asked to call Lucas's name from around the table. Lucas responds by turning his head away from her and then toward her. He makes no sound, in sharp contrast to the smiles and bubbling vocalizations he directs toward the supervisor sitting on the other side of his father. The supervisor, imitating his sounds and body movements, says, "We're having a little conversation." When a doll is set up on the table in front of Lucas, he emits another array of body movements and sounds.*

*During the reflective parent interview, Lucas's vocalizations and loud squeals sing out as he interacts in another part of the room with the direct care practitioner. The supervisor comments to the parents, "We've heard many sounds. What about the cries? Do they mean something more specific, something different from this?" Lucas's mother responds, "Whatever cries he makes, it can always be solved by eating." Lucas's father adds, "We have never noticed any difference in his cries. We just know by the clock."*

In this meeting, the supervisor and direct care practitioner observed a 6-month-old baby who did not vocalize "da," "na," or "ba" or imitate sounds as expected at his age. Moreover, his parents were unable to identify his signals for food or sleep as being specific in any way. Lucas's parents seemed to talk over his head—about him rather than with or to him. After a few weeks in the group care setting, Lucas continued to demonstrate useful coordination of his visual, motor, and cognitive systems. However, his vocalizations had diminished, and at 10 months he was not saying "dada" or "mama" in reference to his parents; he was observed as being overwhelmingly silent. Lucas's mother agreed to have a developmental therapist observe him with the other children and with her when she brought him to the group care setting. A conference between Lucas's mother and the developmental speech therapist opened the way for systematic intervention with Lucas and his mother, which helped them begin to talk with one another. This positive outcome can be traced to the supervisor's and direct care practitioner's observations during the first Visit meeting with this family. The team member's observations alerted them to a possible problem, so they continued to observe for the emergence of Lucas's speech over time. Eventually, these observations led to positive outcomes for Lucas and his family.

Through its emphasis on the identification of systems that the child uses or avoids during the family meeting—and later, on a daily basis—the Visit enables the team and the service system staff to clarify and build on a family's strengths and challenges. The team can also check a child's actions against others in his or her age range by using the Developmental Characteristics Chart. Thus, the Visit guides work with families and serves to link a specific service system with the network of service systems and specialized health care providers qualified to serve families with very young children.

# 7

# SUMMARY

Thus far, this book has described the Visit as a process that provides in-service training for direct care practitioners and fosters change in how service systems view and work with babies, toddlers, and their families. The Visit is woven into the ongoing life of the service system. This integration and the Visit's use of the nonlinear dynamic systems approach to development enables users of the Visit to uncover human potential and build on it. Direct observation, reflection, and synthesis guide the direct care practitioner and his or her supervisor, who work as a team. They follow carefully structured Guides for children 2–36 months of age and develop a coherent picture of the child within the context of his or her family and social-cultural community.

# REFERENCES

Anastasiow, N.J., & Harel, S. (Eds.). (1993). *At-risk infants: Interventions, families, and research.* Baltimore: Paul H. Brookes Publishing Co.

Axtmann, A. (2000). *Informed relationships: The ground for work with infants, toddlers and their families.* Unpublished manuscript.

Berman, C., & Shaw, E. (1996). Family-directed child evaluation and assessment under the Individuals with Disabilities Education Act. In S. Meisels & E. Fenichel (Eds.), *New visions for the developmental assessment of infants and young children* (pp. 361–390). Washington, DC: ZERO TO THREE: National Center for Infants, Toddlers and Families.

Bowlby, J. (1951). Maternal care and mental health. In *World Organization Monograph Series No. 2.* Geneva: World Health Organization.

Brazelton, T.B. (1981). Assessment as a method for enhancing infant development. *Bulletin of the National Center for Clinical Infant Programs, 2,* 1–7.

Bronfenbrenner, U. (1979). *The ecology of human development.* Cambridge, MA: Harvard University Press.

Bulotsky, R. (1995). *Infant initiatives within the parent–child relationship: A child's contribution to development.* Unpublished manuscript.

Call, J. (1995). On becoming a good enough infant. *Infant Mental Health Journal, 16*(1), 52–57.

Eggbeer, L., Mann, T., & Gilkerson, L. (2003, September). Preparing infant–family practitioners: A work in progress. *Zero to Three, 35.*

Emde, R. (1994). Individuality, context, and the search for meaning. *Child Development, 65*(3), 730.

Erikson, E. (1950). *Childhood and society.* New York: W.W. Norton & Company.

Fenichel, E. (Ed.). (1992). *Learning through supervision and mentorship to support the development of infants, toddlers and their families: A source book.* Washington, DC: ZERO TO THREE: National Center for Infants, Toddlers and Families.

Fogel, A., & Thelen, E. (1987). The development of early expressive and communicative action: Re-interpreting the evidence from a dynamic systems perspective. *Developmental Psychology, 23,* 747–761.

Gradel, K., Thompson, M., & Sheehan, R. (1981). Parental and professional agreement in early childhood assessment. *Topics in Early Childhood Special Education, 1*(2), 31–39.

Greenspan, S. (1996). Assessing the emotional and social functioning of infants and young children. In S. Meisels & E. Fenichel (Eds.), *New visions for the developmental assessment of infants and young children* (pp. 231–266). Washington, DC: ZERO TO THREE: National Center for Infants, Toddlers and Families.

Karen, R. (1994). *Becoming attached: Unfolding the mystery of the infant-mother bond and its impact on later life.* New York: Warner Books.

Parmelee, A. (1989). The child's physical health and the development of relationships. In A. Sameroff & R. Emde (Eds.), *Relationship disturbances in early childhood: A developmental approach* (pp. 145–162). New York: Basic Books.

Pawl, J. (1995, February/March). The therapeutic relationship as human connectedness: Being held in another's mind. *Zero to Three*, 3–5.

Provence, S., Erikson, J., Vater, S., & Palermi, S. (Eds.). (1995). *Infant-Toddler Developmental Assessment (IDA).* Chicago: Riverside Publishing.

Rosa, H. (1996). *Assessment instruments for children: Where is the family?* Unpublished manuscript, Teacher's College, Columbia University, New York.

Sander, L.W. (2000). Where are we going in the field of infant mental health? *Infant Mental Health Journal, 21*(1–2), 5–20.

Sekino, Y. (1995). *The empowerment of the parent: Fostering a sense of trust between parent and practitioners.* Unpublished manuscript, Teacher's College, Columbia University, New York.

Thelen, E. (1989). The (re)discovery of motor development: Learning new things from an old field. *Developmental Psychology, 25*(6), 946–949.

Weider, S. (Ed.). (1994). *Diagnostic classification: 0–3 (Diagnostic classification of mental and developmental disorders of infancy and early childhood).* Washington DC: ZERO TO THREE: National Center for Infants, Toddlers and Families.

Winnicott, D.W. (1986). *Home is where we start from: Essays by a psychoanalyst.* New York: W.W. Norton & Company.

# GLOSSARY

**child**  An infant, baby, or toddler ranging in age from 2 to 36 months who participates with his or her family in the Visit.

**comprehensive picture**  A picture of the child and parent together. This is developed during the co-review process as the practitioner team synthesizes the child's self-initiated behaviors, the child's performance of the developmental tasks, the parent's answers to the interview questions, and the parent–child interactions.

**direct care practitioner**  The service practitioner who works most often with the child and his or her family. This person can be a caregiver, home visitor, teacher, family child care provider, paraprofessional, or social services coordinator.

**in the moment**  A term that denotes when the supervisor voices his or her observation of a beneficial parent–child interaction *in the moment* it occurs.

**meeting**  An exchange of information in which all participants (child, parent, direct care practitioner, and supervisor) are equal.

**nonlinear dynamic systems perspective**  A theoretical framework that analyzes how the child coordinates his or her social-emotional, visual, motor, cognitive, and communication systems. Coordination of these systems is grounded in the parent–child relationship and can be observed in the child's behavior. The nonlinear dynamic systems approach does not relate the child's behavior to age as an external marker of the child's performance; rather, it attempts to capture the systems that the child uses in response to the situation.

**parent**  The child's primary caregiver in the home environment (e.g., mother, father, foster parent, grandparent).

**parent–child interaction**  The way the parent and child interact directly and indirectly with one another. The team carefully observes such interactions throughout the meeting to note whether the child and parent seem to notice and respond to one another's requests and mood changes or whether they seem to ignore one another.

These interactions reflect the deeper relationship between child and parent; they enable the practitioner team to begin to understand how the child is—and may not be—developing on a day-by-day basis within the context of the family.

**participant observation** A method of observation used by the supervisor during the meeting with the family. As participant observer, the supervisor withholds his or her inclination to interpret the child's behavior and/or interactions with the parent. He or she interprets these behaviors only after relating them to the context within which they occur. A participant observer may comment on a child's and/or parent's mutually beneficial behavior *in the moment.*

**principles** Ideas about very early child development that are woven throughout the Visit: 1) The child is a complex, dynamic system who perceives and simultaneously initiates his or her actions within the environment; 2) the child develops within the context of the family; 3) the parent is the child's primary caregiver; and 4) the child's family belongs to one or more social-cultural communities.

**reflective parent interview** An interview with the parent that is led by as many of the parent's answers (to the questions noted in the Guides) as relevant. The interview should include pauses to allow the parent to reflect on each question. Some questions may be held back for another time.

**screening** An assessment for possible developmental delays. The Visit may uncover questions that (after discussion with and agreement by the parent) lead to a screening. This more formal assessment can clarify the questions raised by the Visit and in

some cases may provide third-party payment. Examples include the Bayley Scales of Infant Development–Second Edition (BSID-II; Bayley, 1993), the Diagnostic Classification: 0–3 (Diagnostic Classification of Mental and Developmental Disorders of Infancy and Early Childhood; Weider, 1994), and the Infant-Toddler Developmental Assessment (IDA; Provence, Erikson, Vater, & Palermi, 1995).

**separation awareness** Term used during the Visit to describe a child's emotional and physical behaviors when separating or already separated from his or her parent. Although these behaviors can reflect the child's degree of attachment to the parent, further observation beyond the Visit is required.

**service system** A general term indicating the larger system within which a service program is housed. The service program, for example, can be a child care center, foster care setting, family child care home, or homeless shelter program. The individual service program may be administered internally or by the service system of which it is a part.

**supervisor** The person who is ultimately responsible for the family's participation in the service system. The supervisor provides a model for the direct care practitioner as he or she conducts the meeting with the family and the co-review.

**synthesis** Component of the Visit that yields a comprehensive picture of the child within his or her family. During the co-review, the team reflects on, compares, and pieces together what each member has learned by observing the child's self-initiated behaviors, the child's performance of the developmental tasks, the parent's responses to the interview questions, and the team's observations and feelings about the child and parent together.

**tasks** Developmental tasks tailored to a range of ages (within the span of 2–36 months) that elicit social-emotional, visual, motor, cognitive, and communication systems in children. The tasks are administered by the supervisor, and some are preselected for administration by the parent. The supervisor encourages the child to explore and take initiative as he or she attempts to accomplish the task. A nonlinear dynamic systems approach to development allows observation of the child's performance to demonstrate how he or she coordinates the social-emotional, visual, motor, cognitive, and communication systems in the caregiving context. At the same time, the child's performance of the individual task is compared with that of children in the same age range (as described by the Developmental Characteristics Chart), thereby representing a linear approach to development for assessment purposes.

**training** The direct care practitioner's participation in the Visit. The in-service training provided for the direct care practitioner is more aptly labeled as *experience.*

# ANNOTATED BIBLIOGRAPHY

Brazelton, T.B., & Cramer, B.G. (1990). *The earliest relationship: Parents, infants, and the drama of early attachment.* Boston: Addison-Wesley.

This book discusses the development of the parent–child relationships that begin during pregnancy and continue throughout the first few years of life. The importance of parents' expectations and fantasies about their child sets the stage for the attachment process subsequent to the child's birth. The Visit's reflective parent interview questions tap into similar dynamics that relate directly to attachment and parent–child relationships.

Fenichel, E. (Ed.). (1992). *Learning through supervision and mentorship to support the development of infants, toddlers, and their families: A source book.* Washington, DC: ZERO TO THREE: National Center for Infants, Toddlers and Families.

A specific goal of this volume is to help supervisors professionalize the practice of infant care. This goal is accomplished by suggesting ways that supervisors can help staff to understand child development and the needs of young children and to identify their reactions to children and families to establish better working relationships. The process is discussed through case examples and model programs. Regarding the Visit, this book is a particularly good source for helping supervisors refine their role in relation to direct care practitioners.

Fraiberg, S., Adelson, A., & Shapiro, V. (1975). Ghosts in the nursery: A psychoanalytic approach to the problems of impaired infant–mother relationships. *Journal of the American Academy of Child Psychiatry, 14,* 387–427.

Through the use of case examples, this article illustrates how "ghosts," or previous relationships, influence the parent–child relationship. This article uses psychoanalytic theory and technique in a descriptive and uncomplicated manner to help professionals understand how the past affects current and future relationships. These themes may be revealed in the Visit's reflective parent interview and in the practitioners' observations, which are synthesized during the co-review process to inform practice.

Gilkerson, L., & Shahmoon-Shanok, R. (2000). Relationships for growth: Cultivating reflective practice in infant, toddler, and preschool programs. In J. Osofsky & H. Fitzgerald (Eds.), *WAIMH handbook of infant mental health: Vol. 2* (pp. 33–79). New York: John Wiley & Sons.

This chapter presents information about the role of reflective supervision in infant/toddler programs. Based on a survey of program personnel, critical components of reflective supervision are identified, such as providing a supportive holding environment, sharing power, and establishing trust. Benefits for the supervisee, or direct care practitioner, include developing the art of remembering and critical thinking and honing self-knowledge. Programs benefit from quality improvement and accountability. Specific guidelines for implementing reflective supervision are provided. The information from this source is particularly useful for supervisors as they engage in the Visit's co-review process with direct care practitioners.

Gillian, W.S., & Mayes, L.C. (2000). Developmental assessment of infants and toddlers. In C. Zeanah (Ed.), *Handbook of infant mental health* (pp. 236–248). New York: The Guilford Press.

This seminal material clarifies the importance of synthesis in the developmental assessment of infants and toddlers as well as reviews and critiques of developmental assessment instruments. This information is particularly useful because the Visit requires the synthesis (or integration) of observations—of the child's spontaneous behavior, parent–child interactions, and the child's performance of the tasks—with information obtained during the reflective parent interview.

Klass, C.S. (2003). *The home visitor's guidebook: Promoting optimal parent and child development* (2nd ed.). Baltimore: Paul H. Brookes Publishing Co.

This book is a rich compilation of developmental information and advice about working with families and their young children. It may be a valuable resource for home visitors and their supervisors. The book may also be useful to group child care practitioners, family child care practitioners, social services coordinators, and teachers—in short, all service providers who work with families.

Meisels, S.J., & Fenichel, E. (Eds.). (1996). *New visions for the developmental assessment of infants and young children*. Washington, DC: ZERO TO THREE: National Center for Infants, Toddlers and Families.

This book is a collaboration among many disciplines involved in early childhood development and care. Its chapters offer parent perspectives on infant assessment that are important to take into account when conducting the Visit, strategies for interviewing parents, and guidelines for observing children in nonstructured play settings relevant to all aspects of the Visit.

Piaget, J. (1954). *The construction of reality in the child* (M. Cook, Trans.). New York: Ballantine Books.

Piaget asserted how much can be learned by observing the spontaneous behavior of infants. This book uses his observations to illustrate how Piaget came to understand the development of infants' perception of objects and people in space and time. The Visit affords an opportunity for the team members to increase their ability to observe the child's behavior during their meeting with the family and then to reflect on and synthesize these observations during the co-review. These opportunities allow the team members to gain insight into each child and the manner in which infants construct their world.

Porges, S.W. (1993). The infant's sixth sense: Awareness and regulation of bodily processes. *Zero to Three, 14*(2), 12–16.

Consistent with the Visit's principle that infants and toddlers are active participants in their development, this article identifies a terminology to describe inner feeling states that motivate young children to act in their environment. This sixth inner sense, called *interception*, is the foundation of motor, psychological, and social growth. Interception involves sensors within the body that alert the child to feeling states, such as hunger or fatigue, which in turn activate social interaction with caregivers. Understanding such states gives caregivers insight into and language to describe child behaviors, especially those that puzzle adults.

Sander, L.W. (2000). Where are we going in the field of infant mental health? *Infant Mental Health Journal, 21*(1–2), 5–20.

This article provides a context for the Visit by examining changes in the literature, that were based on research policy and have emphasized the importance of the first 3 years of life. These changes include an acceptance of the nonlinear dynamic systems approach to development, the importance of experience and environment on the developing brain, the uncovering of information about critical periods, and the realization that appropriate and timely intervention services are needed.

Sroufe, L.A. (2000). Early relationships and the development of children. *Infant Mental Health Journal, 21*(1–2), 67–74.

This article provides a brief review of attachment theory and research to highlight the importance of early experience in the developing child. The focus on parent–child interactions as the basis of "effective dyadic regulation of arousal and emotion" matches a principle of the Visit—namely, that the child grows and develops within the context of the family.

Thelen, E. (1989). The (re)discovery of motor development: Learning new things from an old field. *Developmental Psychology, 25*(6), 946–949.

This article offers practitioners guidelines on viewing child development as a process rather than as a series of milestones to achieve (the concept embodying most assessment instruments for very young children). The role of context is explained, as children develop skills depending on their environment and experience. This infant–environment interaction is discussed as an "action–perception loop" or a "dialogue," where one informs the other. The article highlights the nonlinear dynamic systems approach to development, which is a core component of the Visit. The article also examines the importance of individual variability in child development, which is a goal of the Visit's co-review process.

Tronick, E.Z. (1986). Interactive mismatch and repair: Challenges to the coping infant. *Zero to Three, 6*(3), 1–6.

This article offers insight into parent–infant interactions. It takes into account both parent and child contributions to this dynamic interplay. The article highlights much of what practitioners observe and discuss during the Visit, such as how the parent or child initiates interaction and how the parent or child responds to complete the circle of communication.

# 8

# User Information
# for the Observation,
# Reflection, Synthesis Guides

The Observation, Reflection, Synthesis Guides (or "Guides") specify how the supervisor and the direct care practitioner can put the Visit into rigorous and, therefore, useful practice. There is one Guide for each of the following age ranges: 2–4, 4–7, 7–10, 10–13, 13–18, 18–24, 24–30, and 30–36 months. These eight Guides are grounded in observation, reflection, and synthesis.

Each Guide begins with a list of materials needed for the age range specific tasks. These materials are everyday objects, with the exception of the 1-inch red cubes. These specific cubes are essential because their dimension and color allow infants and toddlers to perform to their capacity. These cubes are used among many standardized instruments for infants and toddlers. Programs that do not have a set of 1-inch red cubes for assessment purposes can purchase this item directly from Paul H. Brookes Publishing Co. (800-638-3775 or http://www.brookespublishing.com).

Important instructions for the Visit supervisor follow the list of materials. These instructions guide the supervisor through each stage of the Visit.

The Guides also begin with scripts to help the supervisor prepare the direct care practitioner for the Visit and to greet the family and explain the purpose of the meeting. Similar scripts appear throughout each Guide for the supervisor's use with the family and the direct care practitioner.

Observation is the focus during the family's meeting with the practitioner team. Each Guide contains general directions for the team during the meeting and specific directions for observation of parent–child interactions. These recommendations are

51

followed by information about the tasks and the systems that are observed as the child responds to the tasks. As mentioned previously, the systems that the child does not engage when initiating an action are as important to note as the systems that the child actually uses. Specific field-tested cues for administration by the supervisor and the parent parallel the individual systems that will or will not be observed in the child's behavior as he or she responds to each task. (Suggestions that pertain to the parent's participation are set off in italics.) The child can be observed to engage or not engage and coordinate the noted systems when he or she responds to a specific task. The systems listed for each task were observed during the Visit's field trials.

This process of nonevaluative observation enables the supervisor to determine the child's strengths and needs. Except for comments made *in the moment* by the supervisor, the team members' observations are not spoken but are held back until they participate in the co-review stage. (No notes are taken during the family meeting; notes are only recorded by the supervisor during the team's discussion of the meeting during the co-review.)

Reflection is basic to the reflective parent interview. This applies to the first visit with a family and to subsequent visits, which have slightly different questions. During any reflective parent interview, the team observes how the parent maintains a balance between responding to the supervisor's questions and addressing (or ignoring) demands made by the child. Each guide indicates what the team can learn about the parent and the child when asking specific questions. Research conducted with parents at the Center for Infants and Parents has allowed the number and style of the questions to be pared down to allow sufficient time for reflection by the parent.

Observation, reflection, and synthesis are integrated during the co-review. After introducing the direct care practitioner to the co-review process, the supervisor begins the co-review by asking the direct care practitioner questions about parent–child interactions during the meeting, the child's self-initiated behavior, and the child's responses to the tasks. Reflective supervision takes place as the supervisor allows the direct care practitioner's answers to structure the co-review. Distinct review questions are provided to guide the team members as they use a nonlinear dynamic systems perspective to identify the child's strengths and needs in relation to the parent–child interactions. The direct care practitioner and the child do not directly participate in the reflective parent interview (e.g., the direct care practitioner and the child may play in another area of the room). The supervisor uses the co-review to share the parent's answers to the interview questions with the direct care practitioner. In all cases, however, the child's direct care practitioner, parent, and supervisor are present during the reflective parent interview. They can therefore share their observations of parent–child interactions during the interview.

Each Guide offers questions to assist the team members as they synthesize their observations with the parent's responses during the interview. Space is provided throughout the co-review form so that the supervisor can record the observations and ideas that emerge during their co-review of what each has learned from the family. The recorded observations are then available as illustrations to include in the letter to the parent. The Guides also provide three questions to guide the team members as they draft their letter to the parent. Finally, there is a Future Supervision for Direct Care Practitioner Form. This form suggests the areas in which the supervisor might conduct observation and follow-up regarding the direct care practitioner's work.

# MATERIALS FOR THE TASKS

## TO BE PURCHASED FROM BROOKES PUBLISHING

10 red cubes (1 inch x 1 inch x 1 inch)

## EVERYDAY OBJECTS

Ball of any kind (diameter: approximately 9 inches)

Bell or rattle

Cheerios

Child-size plastic spoon

Cloth (one solid color) 18 x 20 inches

Doll with movable legs that can sit in upright position (height: 12 inches)

Jar (height: 3 inches; circumference: 4.5 inches)

Picture book with recognizable objects

Plastic bowl (diameter: 4 inches)

Red yarn ball (diameter: 4 inches)

Rings: three to four red or multicolored rings linked together (diameter of each ring: 2 inches)

Two crayons

Two plastic cups of same color (diameter: 3 inches; height: 2 inches)

Two sheets of 8-inch x 12-inch blank white paper

For directions on how to use these materials, refer to the Cues for Administration column in the Tasks section of each Guide.

**Developmental Characteristics Chart**

| Age (in months) | MOTOR<br>Gross motor<br>Fine motor<br>Manipulative skills | COGNITIVE<br>Visual problem solving<br>Interaction with objects<br>Eye-hand coordination<br>Fine motor<br>Manipulative skills | COMMUNICATION<br>Receptive language<br>Expressive language | SOCIAL-EMOTIONAL<br>Relationship with others<br>Emotion | ADAPTIVE<br>Self-help<br>Self awareness<br>Self-regulation |
|---|---|---|---|---|---|
| 2 | Holds head erect when held upright<br>Demonstrates symmetrical spontaneous movements<br>Keeps hands fisted<br>On belly: lifts head to be aligned with chest | Follows ball symmetrically with eyes and head 30° to either side<br>Stills to the sounds of bell and voice<br>Demonstrates prereaching movements in response to red ring | Attends to voices or bell, coos, cries, and/or grunts | Responds to touch<br>Looks at a person's face<br>Expresses pleasure and discomfort<br>Differentiates between parent and practitioner | Brings hands to mouth<br>Comforts self by sucking thumb or hand |
| 3 | Pull-to-sit position: head lags, assists second time<br>Makes symmetrical spontaneous movements<br>Keeps hands loosely fisted<br>On belly: lifts head to be aligned with chest and pushes up on arms | Follows ball with eyes and head 30°–50°<br>Differentiates between the sound of bell and voice<br>Reaches and makes hand contact with red ring | Vocalizes or stills in response to others' voices or bell<br>Makes musical cooing sounds | Returns eye contact<br>Shows excitement in response to others by moving body | Gazes at and/or plays with hand |
| 4 | Pull-to-sit position: shows some head lag<br>Makes symmetrical spontaneous movements<br>On belly: lifts head high and pushes up on arms<br>Rolls back to side | Follows ball with eyes and head 180°<br>Turns head toward sounds of bell and parent's voice<br>Attends to cube<br>Reaches with open hand(s) for red ring | Initiates vocalization to others and to objects (e.g., toys) | Initiates social contact by smiling or vocalizing | Holds hands together<br>Demonstrates emerging shaping of hand to the shape of an object |
| 5 | Pull-to-sit position: no head lag<br>Rolls back to front<br>Sits with support<br>On belly: lifts head and chest and pushes up on arm | Reaches and grasps cube with palmar grasp | Expresses delight by smiling, babbling, making vowel sounds, or squealing | Shows displeasure at loss of object (e.g., toy) or person | Holds object |

(continued)

*The Visit: Observation, Reflection, Synthesis for Training and Relationship Building,* by Annette Axtmann and Arnegret Dettwiler. © 2005 Paul H. Brookes Publishing Co. All rights reserved.

| Age (in months) | MOTOR | COGNITIVE | COMMUNICATION | SOCIAL-EMOTIONAL | ADAPTIVE |
|---|---|---|---|---|---|
| 6 | Pull-to-sit position: assists head aligned to chest<br>Rolls both ways<br>Sits without support<br>On belly: lifts self onto arms | Transfers cube from one hand to the other<br>Holds cube with palmar grasp while sitting | Vocalizes "da," "ma," and "ba"<br>Imitates sounds | Interacts with others by using smiles and frowns | Reaches out, grasps for, and holds object |
| 7 | Sits unsupported while holding object and makes transition into crawling position<br>Makes the transition from lying on back or belly to sitting | Holds cube with palmar grasp<br>Visually tracks cube when dropped on the floor<br>Bangs cubes together<br>Deliberately uncovers doll or other object of great interest | Vocalizes "dada" and "mama" | Prefers familiar people<br>Pushes away unwanted objects or people<br>Plays social games (e.g., Peekaboo) | Comforts self by bringing object (e.g., pacifier) to mouth |
| 8 | Crawls on hands and knees<br>Pulls to stand by using object or person | Follows falling object<br>Holds cube by opposing thumb from fingers | Responds to "no" | Seeks familiar person when distressed | Feeds self a Cheerio |
| 9 | Pivots while sitting | Bangs cubes together | Balbbles with intonation | Expresses emotion | Holds bottle of juice or milk |
| 10 | Crawls using an alternating pattern<br>Pulls to stand<br>Cruises<br>Stands steadily while holding onto object | Releases cube into cup<br>Uses all fingers to grasp a Cheerio | Says "mama" and "dada" when addressing mother or father | Shows distinct stranger reaction | Finger feeds with help |
| 11 | Cruises<br>Walks forward when pushing a push-toy | Releases cube into cup<br>Dumps Cheerios from cup<br>Picks up a Cheerio with emerging thumb/finger grasp<br>Attempts to imitate scribbling | Says at least one approximation of a word other than "mama" or "dada"<br>Babbles with expression | Plays simple social games (e.g., rolls ball) | Finger feeds well |

*The Visit: Observation, Reflection, Synthesis for Training and Relationship Building,* by Annette Axtmann and Annegret Dettwiler.

| Age (months) | Gross motor | Fine motor | Communication | Social | Adaptive |
|---|---|---|---|---|---|
| 12 | Cruises<br>Stands steadily without support<br>Walks steadily | Dumps cube from cup<br>Dumps Cheerios from cup<br>Uses pincer grasp to secure a Cheerio<br>Imitates scribbling | Says at least one approximation of a word other than "mama" and "dada"<br>Babbles with expression<br>Gestures to indicate needs | Expresses affection with familiar people<br>Plays games (e.g., Pat-a-cake) | Adapts spoon to mouth and brings up spoon to mouth |
| 13 | Walks without support | Intentionally uncovers cube under cup<br>Initiates scribbling<br>Uses pincer grasp to secure a Cheerio<br>Holds crayon with palm at high end | Uses gestures and approximations of words to indicate needs<br>Recognizes names of familiar objects | Indicates discomfort at separation from parents | Manipulates spoon with food<br>Cooperates with dressing |
| 14 | Walks and squats without support | Stacks two cubes<br>Finds cube under reversed cup<br>Places four or five Cheerios in bottle<br>Imitates scribbling<br>Holds crayon at middle | Says two words other than "mama" or "dada"<br>Points to familiar objects or body parts | Hugs parents | Holds and drinks from cup with lid<br>Pulls off socks and shoes |
| 15 | Walks and squats without support | Builds tower of four cubes<br>Imitates drawing a line drawn on a piece of paper<br>Holds crayon at near end | Points to familiar objects or body parts<br>Understands simple instructions | Begins pretend play by feeding doll and imitating | Pulls off pants |
| 18 | Squats steadily<br>Runs<br>Walks up and down steps while holding on and using a symmetrical pattern | Builds a tower of six cubes | Points to and names familiar objects or body parts<br>Says approximately 10 words<br>Follows instructions | Kisses with a puckering motion<br>Says "no"<br>Refuses commands<br>Feeds doll during pretend play | Handles cup and spoon well<br>Attempts to dress self |
| 24 | Walks up and down steps while holding on and using an alternating pattern<br>Runs in a coordinated manner<br>Kicks ball with either leg | Imitates drawn vertical and horizontal strokes<br>Holds crayon with emerging adult-like grasp | Combines words, names of objects, and body parts<br>Follows complex directions | Imitates household activities<br>Engages in pretend play that includes a sequence of words | Dresses self with assistance<br>Uses buttons and snaps independently |

(continued)

*The Visit: Observation, Reflection, Synthesis for Training and Relationship Building*, by Annette Axtmann and Annegret Dettwiler. © 2005 Paul H. Brookes Publishing Co. All rights reserved.

| Age (in months) | MOTOR | COGNITIVE | COMMUNICATION | SOCIAL-EMOTIONAL | ADAPTIVE |
|---|---|---|---|---|---|
| 30 | Walks up and down steps without support<br><br>Jumps<br><br>Kicks ball | Imitates drawn circle<br><br>Holds crayon with adult-like grasp<br><br>Builds structures with cubes (e.g., train) | Combines two to three words<br><br>Asks questions | Helps around the house (e.g., carries a dirty plate to the kitchen sink)<br><br>Takes turns | Puts on shoes<br><br>Feeds self independently |
| 36 | Walks up and down steps without support and using an alternating pattern<br><br>Jumps off floor<br><br>Pedals tricycle | Copies drawn circle or cross<br><br>Holds crayon with adult-like grasp<br><br>Completes simple puzzle | Combines three or more words<br><br>Talks about use of objects<br><br>Understands two prepositions (e.g., "in," "on," "under") | Engages in pretend play with peers | Is toilet trained<br><br>Puts on simple garment independently |

*Source: Yale developmental characteristics and landmarks chart.* (1983). Unpublished document, Yale Child Study Center, New Haven, CT. This chart was developed with the help of Sally Provence, M.D., and Martha Leonard, M.D., faculty at the Yale Child Study Center.

# 9

## OBSERVATION, REFLECTION, SYNTHESIS GUIDES

# Observation, Reflection, Synthesis Guide and Visit Record for

CHILD'S NAME: _____

CHILD'S DATE OF BIRTH: _____

DATE OF VISIT: _____

## AGE RANGE: 2–4 MONTHS

## FOR THE SUPERVISOR

The Visit is an opportunity for you to provide in-service training for caregivers, home visitors, social services coordinators, and family child care providers and for you to strengthen your work with families. These goals will be accomplished through

OBSERVATION    REFLECTION    SYNTHESIS

## PREPARE FOR THE MEETING:

- Review the child's medical record, enrollment form, and/or prior records from the Visit.
- Obtain a blank copy of the appropriate-age Guide by photocopying it from the book or printing it from the accompanying CD-ROM.
- Fill in the child's name throughout the Guide.
- Secure the materials needed for the tasks. These vary according to the child's age range; see the Meeting section of this Guide for the task-specific materials.
- Prioritize the interview questions according to which issues might be most important for the family.
- Consider how the direct care practitioner will be included throughout the meeting with the family.

## DURING THE MEETING:

- Observe interactions among the direct care practitioner, the child, the parent, and, if present, other family members. Be guided by your observations.
- Ask the parent to choose whether to begin with the reflective parent interview or tasks for the child.
- Observe parent–child interactions. Comment *in the moment* on beneficial interactions. Doing so will empower the parent and instruct the direct care practitioner.
- Observe which systems (social-emotional, visual, motor, cognitive, communication) the child uses to solve the task, and how the child solves the task.
- Observe which system(s) the child does not use to solve the task.
- Observe the child's self-initiated behavior and ask yourself how the child's behavior relates to parent–child interactions.
- Pause after each interview question to give the parent time to reflect.
- Do not take notes during the meeting. (Notes can be taken during the co-review.)

## DURING THE CO-REVIEW:

- Ask the direct care practitioner questions as listed in the co-review section of this Guide, and use his or her answers to guide the co-review.
- Share concrete observations, and reflect together on how they relate to
  - The parent–child relationship
  - The child's use of social-emotional, visual, motor, cognitive, and communication systems during tasks
  - The child's self-initiated behavior

*The Visit: Observation, Reflection, Synthesis for Training and Relationship Building*, by Annette Axtmann and Annegret Dettwiler.

- Use the Visit's Developmental Characteristics Chart to compare the child's behavior to that of others in his or her age range.

### SYNTHESIZE:

- Synthesize the parent's responses during the reflective parent interview with observations made by the team during the meeting. Observations should include which systems the child used or did not use and the child's behavior as compared with others in his or her age range.
- Use the synthesis to write a letter for the parent. The letter should summarize what you and the direct care practitioner have learned and how you have agreed with the parent to work for the child's benefit. Illustrate the letter with observations made by you and the direct care practitioner.
- Fill out the Future Supervision for Direct Care Practitioner Form.

*Remember that how you act is as important as what you do.*

# Meeting

## Age Range: 2–4 Months

**Materials:**
Red yarn ball, red or multicolored rings, bell

**Create a space (in the home or child care setting) to administer the Visit:**
Place a blanket on the floor.

**Supervisor to the direct care practitioner:**

*You are here to exchange information with the family because you provide direct care for the child—meaning that the family considers you a very important person in the service system. There are two parts to our meeting with the family: 1) tasks for the child and 2) a reflective parent interview. During the interview, allow the child to explore and to interact with his or her parent naturally. Please allow the child to cry, crawl, or walk to establish contact with his or her parent. Do not pull the child back or ask the parent for help. We want to observe how the parent responds—or does not respond—to the child while answering sensitive questions. We need to observe how the parent and child interact because the child's growth and development depend on parent–child interactions.*

**Supervisor to the parent:**

*Welcome. You were asked to participate in this meeting so that we can exchange information and share the care of your child with you. We will administer some developmental tasks to determine _____'s individual competencies. As you are part of _____'s family, we will ask you some questions about him or her. Please care for _____ or ask the direct care practitioner to do so when you feel it is best. We will observe how you interact with _____ so that we can perhaps imitate you while we are caring for him or her. This meeting takes approximately 30 minutes. Would you prefer to begin with the interview questions or the tasks?*

**Overall directions for the supervisor during the meeting:**
- Remember that observations are nonevaluative; they will be interpreted and discussed during the co-review.
- Ask all participants to sit on the floor, at the child's eye level.
- Observe the child's eye contact, smiles, and vocalizations.
- Compare the child's reactions to his or her parent (as a familiar person) and to you (as a stranger).
- Observe and comment on the competence expressed by the child's self-initiated behaviors.

- Ask the parent to administer the tasks that are italicized in the chart, and do not interfere when the parent administers a task.
- If the child does not do a task, ask the parent if the child does it at home.

**WHAT TO LOOK FOR DURING PARENT–CHILD INTERACTIONS:**
- Clarity of the child's behavior toward the parent (e.g., eye contact, vocalizations, body movement)
- Contingent parent responses to the child
- Noncontingent parent responses to the child
- No parent response to the child (i.e., the parent ignores the child)
- Child self-initiated actions (i.e., whether the parent permits them)
- Cultural aspects of parent–child interactions

## TASKS
### GUIDELINES FOR ADMINISTERING AND OBSERVING PERFORMANCE OF THE TASKS

| Task and related systems | Cues for administration | Strengths and needs to observe as the child responds to the tasks |
| --- | --- | --- |
| **Engages in activity on back** Communication Visual Social-emotional Motor | *Ask the parent to place the child on his or her back and to talk to the child.* Talk to and smile at the child. Observe any differences in the child's reaction while the parent talks and while you talk. | Vocalization Eye contact Symmetry of posture and movement Expression of affect |
| **Demonstrates visual tracking** Cognitive Visual Motor | Hold the yarn ball 12 inches from the child's face. Move the yarn ball and your face horizontally across the child's visual field. Observe the child's turning of his or her eyes and head. | Visual recognition and tracking of object Symmetry of head rotation Eye–head coordination |
| **Responds to the rings** Visual Motor Cognitive | Hold the rings in a vertical line at mid-line, within the child's reach. Allow the child to respond to the rings. Move the rings if necessary to encourage the child's reaching movements and possible grasping of the rings. | Coordination of visual and motor systems (eye–hand coordination) Symmetry of reaching Emerging shaping of hand to ring (adaptive) |

| Task and related systems | Cues for administration | Strengths and needs to observe as the child responds to the tasks |
|---|---|---|
| **Responds to the bell and voices**<br>Communication<br>Cognitive<br>Social-emotional<br>Motor<br>Visual | *Ask the parent to move out of the child's field of vision.*<br>*Ask the parent to ring the bell.*<br>*Ask the parent to call the child's name.* | Sound recognition<br>Sound differentiation<br>Expression of affect |
| **Pulls to sit**<br>Visual<br>Motor<br>Social-emotional<br>Cognitive | *Ask the parent to place the child on his or her back.*<br>Place the child's feet against your body.<br>Place your thumbs into the palms of the child's hands and wrap your fingers around the back of the child's hands.<br>Allow the child to participate in pulling to a sitting position.<br>Repeat the task, and observe whether the child helps you. | Eye contact<br>Alignment of head with trunk<br>Grasping function |
| **Engages in activity on belly**<br>Visual<br>Motor<br>Cognitive<br>Social-emotional | *Ask the parent to place the child on his or her belly.*<br>Observe how the child lifts his or her head and chest and pushes up on his or her arms.<br>Place your face at the level of the child's face and talk to him or her if encouragement is necessary for the child to lift his or her head. | Symmetry of posture and movement |

# REFLECTIVE PARENT INTERVIEW

## QUESTIONS FOR THE FIRST VISIT

Please use the following script as a guide only. Prioritize the order of the questions according to what you already know and are learning about the child and parent during this meeting with them. Wait for the parent to reflect and to respond fully—in whatever way seems comfortable for him or her. Remember that some questions can be left for later during the family's participation in the program. As you ask questions, observe how the parent maintains a balance between responding to the questions and to the demands made by the child. **Do not take notes.**

| INTERVIEW AREA | QUESTION(S) |
|---|---|
| Family beginnings | *How did you begin as a family?* |
| Role as a parent | *How did you feel when you found out you were going to be a parent? Did you plan to have _____?* |
| Pregnancy and delivery | *How did the pregnancy go? What was the delivery like?* |
| Family supports | *What was it like for you when you first came home with _____?* |
| Parent's understanding of the child's cues | *How does _____ tell you that he or she is hungry or tired? Please describe or mimic _____'s cries or signals regarding hunger or sleep.* |
| Separation | *Have you and _____ ever been separated? Who else has cared for (or cares for, if ongoing) your child? When? How did (or do) you feel about this?* |
| Intergenerational issues, culture, and values | *Are you raising _____ in the same way that you were raised or in a different way? Do you follow your parents' customs? What languages do you speak at home?* |
| Caregiving needs | *What are _____'s special needs?* |

## CLOSURE OF THE MEETING

*There is much more for us to learn from one another. We will write you a letter summarizing what we have learned about _____ and how we all have agreed to work with him or her. We appreciate the time that you and _____ have spent with us. Thank you.*

*The Visit: Observation, Reflection, Synthesis for Training and Relationship Building*, by Annette Axtmann and Annegret Dettwiler.

# REFLECTIVE PARENT INTERVIEW

## QUESTIONS FOR SUBSEQUENT VISITS

Please use the following script as a guide only. Prioritize the order of the questions according to what you already know and are learning about the child and parent during this meeting with them. Wait for the parent to reflect and to respond fully—in whatever way seems comfortable for him or her. Remember that some questions can be left for later during the family's participation in the program. As you ask questions, observe how the parent maintains a balance between responding to the questions and to the demands made by the child. **Do not take notes.**

| INTERVIEW AREA | QUESTION(S) |
|---|---|
| Family relationships | *How are things going at home?* |
| Role as a parent | *How do you feel now that you have been a parent for a while?* |
| Child's ongoing health and development | *Do you have any new concerns about _____'s health or development?* |
| Family supports | *Is your family supporting you? If so, how?* |
| Parent's understanding of the child's cues | *Have you noticed any changes in the way that _____ lets you know what he or she wants or needs? Have you made any changes in the way that you are responding to _____?* |
| Relationship with the program | *How has _____ been responding to the way that we are working with him or her? Have you felt included?* |
| Intergenerational issues, culture, and values | *What kinds of things are you and _____ doing together at home? Are you raising _____ in the same way that you were raised or in a different way?* |
| Caregiving needs | *Does _____ have any special needs at this time?* |

## CLOSURE OF THE MEETING

*There is much more for us to learn from one another. We will write you a letter summarizing what we have learned about _____ and how we all have agreed to work with him (or her). We appreciate the time that you and _____ have spent with us. Thank you.*

## CO-REVIEW OF VISIT # _____
## FOR CHILD'S ONGOING RECORD

CHILD'S NAME: _____

DATE OF VISIT: _____

CHILD'S AGE AT TIME OF VISIT (IN MONTHS AND DAYS): _____

TEAM MEMBERS:  SUPERVISOR _____

DIRECT CARE PRACTITIONER _____

NAME(S) OF CHILD'S FAMILY MEMBER(S) IN ATTENDANCE: _____

_____

_____

HEALTH ISSUES NOTED ON CHILD'S MEDICAL FORM: _____

_____

_____

**2–4 MONTHS**

**MATERIALS:**

Pencil, Developmental Characteristics Chart

**SUPERVISOR INTRODUCES THE CO-REVIEW TO THE DIRECT CARE PRACTITIONER:**

*During this co-review, we will share our observations of the child and his or her parent. We will relate these observations to what each of us remembers about the child's response to his or her parent and to us, the child's self-initiated behaviors, the child's performance of the tasks, and the parent's answers during the interview. In addition, we will record observations of parent–child interactions in the right-hand column of the chart that follows. Overall, we will ask the following questions during this co-review:*

- *What do the observations indicate about the child's strengths and/or needs? How were these areas of strength or need influenced by the child's interactions with his or her parent?*
- *Which systems did the child use or not use to solve the tasks?*
- *Did the child's behavior during the meeting indicate that the child's systems are in balance or off balance?*

*As we synthesize this information, we will develop a picture of the child within the context of his or her family. We will use this picture to draft a letter to the parent summarizing what we and the parent agreed to do for the child's well-being. We will illustrate the letter with our observations.*

## CHILD'S STRENGTHS AND NEEDS

**SUPERVISOR TO THE DIRECT CARE PRACTITIONER:**

*We will share our observations of how the child used his or her various systems to solve each task. This will enable us to uncover the child's strengths. If the parent reported that he or she has seen the child do the task at home, we will note that here as well.*

*The Visit: Observation, Reflection, Synthesis for Training and Relationship Building,* by Annette Axtmann and Annegret Dettwiler.

| Task and related systems | Observations of how the child used his or her systems | Observations of parent–child interactions during the task |
|---|---|---|
| **Engages in activity on back**<br>Communication<br>Visual<br>Social-emotional<br>Motor | Did the child smile and/or vocalize?<br>Were the child's posture and spontaneous movements symmetrical?<br>How did the child respond to his or her position?<br>Did the child differentiate between the parent and you? | |
| **Demonstrates visual tracking**<br>Cognitive<br>Visual<br>Motor | Did the child turn his or her eyes and head horizontally to follow the yarn ball?<br>Did the child follow your face? | |
| **Responds to the rings**<br>Visual<br>Motor<br>Cognitive | Did the child purposely move his or her arms in the direction of the rings?<br>Did the child visually focus on the rings?<br>Did the child touch and grasp the rings?<br>Did the child involve both hands in the reaching activity? | |
| **Responds to the bell and voices**<br>Communication<br>Cognitive<br>Social-emotional<br>Motor<br>Visual | Did the child's use of body movements demonstrate differentiation of sounds?<br>Did the child demonstrate facial affect or vocalize?<br>Did the child turn toward the sound of the bell or the parent's voice? | |
| **Pulls to sit**<br>Visual<br>Motor<br>Social-emotional<br>Cognitive | Did the child make eye contact?<br>Did the child actively grasp your thumbs?<br>Did the child assist more on the second trial?<br>How did the child align his or her head with his or her body? | |

*The Visit: Observation, Reflection, Synthesis for Training and Relationship Building,* by Annette Axtmann and Annegret Dettwiler.

**2–4 MONTHS**

| Task and related systems | Observations of how the child used his or her systems | Observations of parent–child interactions during the task |
| --- | --- | --- |
| **Engages in activity on belly**<br>Visual<br>Motor<br>Cognitive<br>Social-emotional | Did the child lift his or her head and chest?<br>How did the child control his or her head?<br>Did the child push up with his or her arms, with his or her hands open?<br>Did the child respond socially? | |

SUPERVISOR TO THE DIRECT CARE PRACTITIONER:

- *What are the child's strengths, and how do they seem to relate to our observations of parent–child interactions?*
- *Did the parent and child interact during the tasks, and did these interactions influence the child's performance of the tasks?*
- *Did the parent seem to understand the child's behavior?*
- *Did the parent's response mesh with the child's behavior?*
- *Did the parent ignore the child?*
- *Did the parent allow the child to self-initiate?*
- *Does it appear that the family's culture influenced interactions between the parent and child and the child's use of his or her systems?*

*Let's use the Developmental Characteristics Chart to compare the child's task performance with that of other children in the same age range. What do we learn from the comparisons?*

*The Visit: Observation, Reflection, Synthesis for Training and Relationship Building,* by Annette Axtmann and Annegret Dettwiler.

# REFLECTIVE PARENT INTERVIEW FOR THE FIRST VISIT

## SUPERVISOR TO THE DIRECT CARE PRACTITIONER:

*What seemed most important in the parent's responses to the questions? We will write these replies in the child's record. Did the parent interact with the child during the interview? If so, we will need to describe these interactions in the child's record as well.*

| Interview area | Question(s) | Notes and observations |
|---|---|---|
| Family beginnings | How did you begin as a family? | |
| Role as a parent | How did you feel when you found out you were going to be a parent? Did you plan to have _____? | |
| Pregnancy and delivery | How did the pregnancy go? What was the delivery like? | |
| Family supports | What was it like for you when you first came home with _____? | |
| Parent's understanding of the child's cues | How does _____ tell you that he or she is hungry or tired? Please describe or mimic _____'s cries or signals regarding hunger or sleep. | |
| Separation | Have you and _____ ever been separated? Who else cared for (or cares for, if ongoing) your child? When? How did (or do) you feel about this? | |
| Intergenerational issues, culture, and values | Are you raising _____ in the same way that you were raised or in a different way? Do you follow your parents' customs? What languages do you speak at home? | |
| Caregiving needs | What are _____'s special needs? | |

**2–4 MONTHS**

# REFLECTIVE PARENT INTERVIEW FOR SUBSEQUENT VISITS

**SUPERVISOR TO THE DIRECT CARE PRACTITIONER:**

*What seemed most important in the parent's responses to the questions? We will write these replies in the child's record. Did the parent interact with the child during the interview? If so, we will need to describe these interactions in the child's chart as well.*

| Interview area | Question(s) | Notes and observations |
|---|---|---|
| Family relationships | How are things going at home? | |
| Role as a parent | How do you feel now that you have been a parent for a while? | |
| Child's ongoing health and development | Do you have any new concerns about _____'s health or development? | |
| Family supports | Is your family supporting you? If so, how? | |
| Parent's understanding of the child's cues | Have you noticed any changes in the way that _____ lets you know what he or she wants or needs? Have you made any changes in the way that you are responding to _____? | |
| Relationship with the child care program | How has _____ been responding to the way that we are working with him or her? Have you felt included? | |
| Intergenerational issues, culture, and values | What kinds of things are you and _____ doing together at home? Are you raising _____ in the same way that you were raised or in a different way? | |
| Caregiving needs | Does _____ have any special needs at this time? | |

*The Visit: Observation, Reflection, Synthesis for Training and Relationship Building,* by Annette Axtmann and Annegret Dettwiler.

# SYNTHESIS

**SUPERVISOR TO THE DIRECT CARE PRACTITIONER:**

*We will now synthesize our observations from the meeting with the information gained during the reflective parent interview to address four areas in the spaces that follow. The answers to these questions, illustrated by our concrete observations, structure the letter for the parent.*

1.  How did the child demonstrate strengths in his or her responses to the tasks, to the parent, and to us? How did the child coordinate his or her systems, and did the child initiate without prompting from the parent or supervisor?

2.  How were these behaviors related to the interactions that we observed between the parent and child? How did the child contribute to these interactions?

**2–4 MONTHS**

3. Does the parent have any special concerns? How did we agree with the parent to respond to these concerns?

4. Are we concerned about the child's development in any way? If so, how can we suggest working with the family to strengthen the child's development within his or her social-cultural community?

*The Visit: Observation, Reflection, Synthesis for Training and Relationship Building*, by Annette Axtmann and Annegret Dettwiler.

# Closure

## Supervisor to the direct care practitioner:

*How do you feel about working with this family?*

*I will transform our notes into the letter for the parent. Once you read and approve the letter, I'll ask you to sign it as well. Please let me know what you continue to observe on a daily basis. We will meet again to reflect together on this family and what we have learned about the family today, as well as what you are observing on a daily basis.*

NAME OF PRACTITIONER: _____

DATE OF VISIT: _____

NUMBER OF VISIT FOR PRACTITIONER: _____

CHILD'S AND PARENT'S NAMES: _____

_____

_____

The following sections detail the direct care practitioner's areas of strength and areas for future observation and follow-up.

## DURING THE MEETING

Observe the child and parent before interacting with them; this will allow your behavior to be tuned to the child and parent.

| Areas of strength | Areas for future observation and follow-up |
|---|---|
|  |  |

Reflect before answering questions posed by the supervisor and illustrate answers (in part) with nonevaluative observations.

| Areas of strength | Areas for future observation and follow-up |
|---|---|
|  |  |

Describe systems used and/or systems not used by the child during tasks and during self-initiated behavior.

| Areas of strength | Areas for future observation and follow-up |
|---|---|
|  |  |

Relate observations to the child's history as told by the parent during the reflective parent interview (or related by the supervisor) that contribute to the synthesis of information collected from child and parent during the meeting.

| Areas of strength | Areas for future observation and follow-up |
|---|---|
|  |  |

*The Visit: Observation, Reflection, Synthesis for Training and Relationship Building*, by Annette Axtmann and Annegret Dettwiler.

Suggest one or two ways—based on observations and synthesis—to work with the family.

| Areas of strength | Areas for future observation and follow-up |
|---|---|
|  |  |

Relate knowledge of the nonlinear dynamic systems perspective of child development and basic principles of development to aspects of the child's and/or parent's behavior.

| Areas of strength | Areas for future observation and follow-up |
|---|---|
|  |  |

## OBSERVATION, REFLECTION, SYNTHESIS GUIDE AND VISIT RECORD FOR

CHILD'S NAME: _____

CHILD'S DATE OF BIRTH: _____

DATE OF VISIT: _____

## AGE RANGE: 4–7 MONTHS

## FOR THE SUPERVISOR

The Visit is an opportunity for you to provide in-service training for caregivers, home visitors, social services coordinators, and family child care providers and for you to strengthen your work with families. These goals will be accomplished through

OBSERVATION    REFLECTION    SYNTHESIS

### PREPARE FOR THE MEETING:

- Review the child's medical record, enrollment form, and/or prior records from the Visit.
- Obtain a blank copy of the appropriate-age Guide by photocopying it from the book or printing it from the accompanying CD-ROM.
- Fill in the child's name throughout the Guide.
- Secure the materials needed for the tasks. These vary according to the child's age range; see the Meeting section of this Guide for the task-specific materials.
- Prioritize the interview questions according to which issues might be most important for the family.
- Consider how the direct care practitioner will be included throughout the meeting with the family.

### DURING THE MEETING:

- Observe interactions among the direct care practitioner, the child, the parent, and, if present, other family members. Be guided by your observations.
- Ask the parent to choose whether to begin with the reflective parent interview or tasks for the child.
- Observe parent–child interactions. Comment *in the moment* on beneficial interactions. Doing so will empower the parent and instruct the direct care practitioner.
- Observe which systems (social-emotional, visual, motor, cognitive, communication) the child uses to solve the task, and how the child solves the task.
- Observe which system(s) the child does not use to solve the task.
- Observe the child's self-initiated behavior and ask yourself how the child's behavior relates to parent–child interactions.
- Pause after each interview question to give the parent time to reflect.
- Do not take notes during the meeting. (Notes can be taken during the co-review.)

### DURING THE CO-REVIEW:

- Ask the direct care practitioner questions as listed in the co-review section of this Guide, and use his or her answers to guide the co-review.
- Share concrete observations, and reflect together on how they relate to
  - The parent–child relationship
  - The child's use of social-emotional, visual, motor, cognitive, and communication systems during tasks
  - The child's self-initiated behavior

---

**4–7 MONTHS**

2

- Use the Visit's Developmental Characteristics Chart to compare the child's behavior to that of others in his or her age range.

### SYNTHESIZE:

- Synthesize the parent's responses during the reflective parent interview with observations made by the team during the meeting. Observations should include which systems the child used or did not use and the child's behavior as compared with others in his or her age range.
- Use the synthesis to write a letter for the parent. The letter should summarize what you and the direct care practitioner have learned and how you have agreed with the parent to work for the child's benefit. Illustrate the letter with observations made by you and the direct care practitioner.
- Fill out the Future Supervision for Direct Care Practitioner Form.

*Remember that how you act is as important as what you do.*

# MEETING
## AGE RANGE: 4–7 MONTHS

**MATERIALS:**

Yarn ball, bell, red or multicolored rings, cube

**CREATE A SPACE (IN THE HOME OR CHILD CARE SETTING) TO ADMINISTER THE VISIT:**

Place a blanket on the floor. Clear a space on an adult-size table.

**SUPERVISOR TO THE DIRECT CARE PRACTITIONER:**

*You are here to exchange information with the family because you provide direct care for the child—meaning that the family considers you a very important person in the service system. There are two parts to our meeting with the family: 1) tasks for the child and 2) a reflective parent interview. During the interview, allow the child to explore and to interact with his or her parent naturally. Please allow the child to cry, crawl, or walk to establish contact with his or her parent. Do not pull the child back or ask the parent for help. We want to observe how the parent responds—or does not respond—to the child while he or she is answering sensitive questions. We need to observe how the parent and child interact because the child's growth and development depend on parent–child interactions.*

**SUPERVISOR TO THE PARENT:**

*Welcome. You were asked to participate in this meeting so that we can exchange information and share the care of your child with you. We will administer some developmental tasks to determine _____'s individual competencies. As you are part of _____'s family, we will ask you some questions about him or her. Please care for _____ or ask the direct care practitioner to do so when you feel it is best. We will observe how you interact with _____ so that we can perhaps imitate you while we are caring for him or her. This meeting takes approximately 30 minutes. Would you prefer to begin with the interview questions or the tasks?*

**OVERALL DIRECTIONS FOR THE SUPERVISOR DURING THE MEETING:**

- Remember that observations are nonevaluative; they will be interpreted and discussed during the co-review.
- Ask all to participants to sit on the floor, at the child's eye level.
- Observe the child's eye contact, smiles, and vocalizations.
- Compare the child's reactions to his or her parent (as a familiar person) and to you (as a stranger).
- Observe and comment on the competence expressed by the child's self-initiated behaviors.

*The Visit: Observation, Reflection, Synthesis for Training and Relationship Building,* by Annette Axtmann and Annegret Dettwiler.

- Ask the parent to administer the tasks that are italicized in the chart, and do not interfere when the parent administers a task.
- If the child does not do a task, ask the parent if the child does it at home.

### WHAT TO LOOK FOR DURING PARENT–CHILD INTERACTIONS:
- Clarity of the child's behavior toward the parent (e.g., eye contact, vocalizations, body movement)
- Contingent parent responses to the child
- Noncontingent parent responses to the child
- No parent response to the child (i.e., parent ignores the child)
- Child self-initiated actions (i.e., whether the parent permits them)
- Cultural aspects of parent–child interactions

## TASKS
### GUIDELINES FOR ADMINISTERING AND OBSERVING PERFORMANCE OF THE TASKS

| Task and related systems | Cues for administration | Strengths and needs to observe as the child responds to the tasks |
|---|---|---|
| **Engages in activity on back**<br>Communication<br>Visual<br>Social-emotional<br>Motor | *Ask the parent to place the child on his or her back and to talk to the child.*<br>Talk to and smile at the child.<br>Observe for differences in the child's reaction while the parent talks and while you talk. | Vocalization<br>Eye contact<br>Symmetry of posture and movement<br>Expression of affect |
| **Demonstrates visual tracking**<br>Cognitive<br>Visual<br>Motor | Hold the yarn ball 12 inches from the child's face.<br>Move the yarn ball and your face horizontally across the child's visual field.<br>Observe the child's turning of his or her eyes and head. | Visual recognition and tracking of object<br>Symmetry of head rotation<br>Eye–head coordination |
| **Responds to the rings**<br>Visual<br>Motor<br>Cognitive | Hold the rings in a vertical line at mid-line, within the child's reach.<br>Allow the child to respond to the rings.<br>Move the rings if necessary to encourage the child's reaching movements and possible grasping of the rings. | Coordination of visual and motor systems (eye–hand coordination)<br>Symmetry of reaching and grasping (adaptive skills) |

*The Visit: Observation, Reflection, Synthesis for Training and Relationship Building*, by Annette Axtmann and Annegret Dettwiler.

**4–7 MONTHS**

| Task and related systems | Cues for administration | Strengths and needs to observe as the child responds to the tasks |
|---|---|---|
| **Responds to the bell and voices**<br>Communication<br>Cognitive<br>Social-emotional<br>Motor<br>Visual | *Ask the parent to move out of the child's field of vision.*<br>*Ask the parent to ring the bell.*<br>*Ask the parent to call the child's name.* | Sound recognition<br>Sound differentiation<br>Expression of affect |
| **Pulls to sit**<br>Visual<br>Motor<br>Social-emotional<br>Cognitive | *Ask the parent to place the child on his or her back.*<br>Place the child's feet against your body.<br>Place your thumbs into the palms of the child's hands and wrap your fingers around the back of the child's hands.<br>Secure eye contact with the child.<br>Allow the child to participate in pulling to a sitting position.<br>Repeat the task, and observe whether the child helps you.<br>Observe whether the child sits with or without support. | Eye contact<br>Alignment of head with trunk<br>Grasping function |
| **Engages in activity on belly**<br>Visual<br>Motor<br>Cognitive<br>Social-emotional | *Ask the parent to place the child on his or her belly.*<br>Observe how the child lifts his or her head and chest and pushes up on his or her arms.<br>Place your face at the level of the child's face and talk to him or her if encouragement is necessary for the child to lift his or her head. | Symmetry of posture and movement<br>Expression of affect |
| **Rolls**<br>Cognitive<br>Visual<br>Motor | Encourage the child to roll by placing the rings at the child's eye level, out of reach.<br>Observe how the child attempts to roll over. | Coordination of visual and motor systems |
| **Grasps a cube**<br>Visual<br>Cognitive<br>Motor | *Ask the parent to sit at the table with the child on his or her lap so that the child is facing the table. (This task can be done on the floor if the family prefers.)*<br>Place one cube within the child's reach on the table or in the palm of the parent's hand.<br>Give the child time to grasp the cube.<br>Drop the cube on the floor. | Visual recognition of object<br>Eye–hand coordination<br>Shaping of hand to object (type of grasp) |

*The Visit: Observation, Reflection, Synthesis for Training and Relationship Building,* by Annette Axtmann and Annegret Dettwiler.

# Reflective Parent Interview

## Questions for the First Visit

Please use the following script as a guide only. Prioritize the order of the questions according to what you already know and are learning about the child and parent during this meeting with them. Wait for the parent to reflect and to respond fully—in whatever way seems comfortable for him or her. Remember that some questions can be left for later during the family's participation in the program. As you ask questions, observe how the parent maintains a balance between responding to the questions and to the demands made by the child. **Do not take notes.**

| Interview area | Question(s) |
|---|---|
| Family beginnings | *How did you begin as a family?* |
| Role as a parent | *How did you feel when you found out you were going to be a parent? Did you plan to have _____?* |
| Pregnancy and delivery | *How did the pregnancy go? What was the delivery like?* |
| Family supports | *What was it like for you when you first came home with _____?* |
| Parent's understanding of the child's cues | *How does _____ tell you that he or she is hungry or tired? Please describe or mimic _____'s cries or signals regarding hunger or sleep.* |
| Separation | *Have you and _____ ever been separated? Who else has cared for (or cares for, if ongoing) your child? When? How did (or do) you feel about this?* |
| Intergenerational issues, culture, and values | *Are you raising _____ in the same way that you were raised or in a different way? Do you follow your parents' customs? What languages do you speak at home?* |
| Caregiving needs | *What are _____'s special needs?* |

## Closure of the Meeting

*There is much more for us to learn from one another. We will write you a letter summarizing what we have learned about _____ and how we all have agreed to work with him (or her). We appreciate the time that you and _____ have spent with us. Thank you.*

# REFLECTIVE PARENT INTERVIEW

## QUESTIONS FOR SUBSEQUENT VISITS

Please use the following script as a guide only. Prioritize the order of the questions according to what you already know and are learning about the child and parent during this meeting with them. Wait for the parent to reflect and to respond fully—in whatever way seems comfortable for him or her. Remember that some questions can be left for later during the family's participation in the program. As you ask questions, observe how the parent maintains a balance between responding to the questions and to the demands made by the child. **Do not take notes.**

| INTERVIEW AREA | QUESTION(S) |
|---|---|
| Family relationships | *How are things going at home?* |
| Role as a parent | *How do you feel now that you have been a parent for a while?* |
| Child's ongoing health and development | *Do you have any new concerns about _____'s health or development?* |
| Family supports | *Is your family supporting you? If so, how?* |
| Parent's understanding of the child's cues | *Have you noticed any changes in the way that _____ lets you know what he or she wants or needs? Have you made any changes in the way that you are responding to _____?* |
| Relationship with the program | *How has _____ been responding to the way that we are working with him or her? Have you felt included?* |
| Intergenerational issues, culture, and values | *What kinds of things are you and _____ doing together at home? Are you raising _____ in the same way that you were raised or in a different way?* |
| Caregiving needs | *Does _____ have any special needs at this time?* |

## CLOSURE OF THE MEETING

*There is much more for us to learn from one another. We will write you a letter summarizing what we have learned about _____ and how we all have agreed to work with him (or her). We appreciate the time that you and _____ have spent with us. Thank you.*

*The Visit: Observation, Reflection, Synthesis for Training and Relationship Building*, by Annette Axtmann and Annegret Dettwiler.

## CO-REVIEW OF VISIT # _____
## FOR CHILD'S ONGOING RECORD

CHILD'S NAME: _____

DATE OF VISIT: _____

CHILD'S AGE AT TIME OF VISIT (IN MONTHS AND DAYS): _____

TEAM MEMBERS: SUPERVISOR _____

DIRECT CARE PRACTITIONER _____

NAME(S) OF CHILD'S FAMILY MEMBER(S) IN ATTENDANCE: _____

_____

_____

HEALTH ISSUES NOTED ON CHILD'S MEDICAL FORM: _____

_____

_____

**4–7 MONTHS**

**MATERIALS:**
Pencil, Developmental Characteristics Chart

**SUPERVISOR INTRODUCES THE CO-REVIEW TO THE DIRECT CARE PRACTITIONER:**

*During this co-review, we will share our observations of the child and his or her parent. We will relate these observations to what each of us remembers about the child's response to his or her parent and to us, the child's self-initiated behaviors, the child's performance of the tasks, and the parent's answers during the interview. In addition, we will record observations of parent–child interactions in the right-hand column of the chart that follows. Overall, we will ask the following questions during this co-review:*

- *What do the observations indicate about the child's strengths and/or needs? How were these areas of strength or need influenced by the child's interactions with his or her parent?*
- *Which systems did the child use or not use to solve the tasks?*
- *Did the child's behavior during the meeting indicate that the child's systems are in balance or off balance?*

*As we synthesize this information, we will develop a picture of the child within the context of his or her family. We will use this picture to draft a letter to the parent summarizing what we and the parent agreed to do for the child's well-being. We will illustrate the letter with our observations.*

## CHILD'S STRENGTHS AND NEEDS

**SUPERVISOR TO THE DIRECT CARE PRACTITIONER:**

*We will share our observations of how the child used his or her various systems to solve each task. This will enable us to uncover the child's strengths. If the parent reported that he or she has seen the child do the task at home, we will note that here as well.*

| Task and related systems | Observations of how the child used his or her systems | Observations of parent–child interactions during the task |
|---|---|---|
| **Engages in activity on back**<br>Communication<br>Visual<br>Social-emotional<br>Motor | Did the child smile and/or vocalize?<br>Were the child's posture and spontaneous movements symmetrical?<br>How did the child respond to his or her position?<br>Did the child differentiate between the parent and you? | |
| **Demonstrates visual tracking**<br>Cognitive<br>Visual<br>Motor | Did the child turn his or her eyes and head horizontally to follow the yarn ball?<br>Did the child follow your face? | |
| **Responds to the rings**<br>Visual<br>Motor<br>Cognitive | Did the child purposely move his or her arms in the direction of the rings?<br>Did the child visually focus on the rings?<br>Did the child touch and grasp the rings?<br>Did the child involve both hands in the reaching activity? | |
| **Responds to the bell and voices**<br>Communication<br>Cognitive<br>Social-emotional<br>Motor<br>Visual | Did the child's use of body movements demonstrate differentiation of sounds?<br>Did the child demonstrate facial affect or vocalize?<br>Did the child turn toward the sound of the bell or the parent's voice? | |
| **Pulls to sit**<br>Visual<br>Motor<br>Social-emotional<br>Cognitive | Did the child make eye contact?<br>Did the child actively grasp your thumbs?<br>Did the child assist more on the second trial?<br>How did the child align his or her head with his or her body? | |

| Task and related systems | Observations of how the child used his or her systems | Observations of parent–child interactions during the task |
| --- | --- | --- |
| **Engages in activity on belly**<br>Visual<br>Motor<br>Cognitive<br>Social-emotional | Did the child lift his or her head and chest?<br>How did the child control his or her head?<br>Did the child push up with his or her arms, with his or her hands open?<br>Did the child respond socially? | |
| **Rolls**<br>Cognitive<br>Visual<br>Motor | Did the child roll from his or her belly to back?<br>Did the child roll from his or her back to belly? | |
| **Grasps a cube**<br>Visual<br>Cognitive<br>Motor | Did the child look at the cube?<br>Did the child reach for and grasp the cube with his or her whole hand?<br>Did the child transfer the cube from hand to hand?<br>Did the child follow the cube when it dropped on the floor? | |

Supervisor to the direct care practitioner:

- *What are the child's strengths, and how do they seem to relate to our observations of parent–child interactions?*
- *Did the parent and child interact during the tasks, and did these interactions influence the child's performance of the tasks?*
- *Did the parent seem to understand the child's behavior?*
- *Did the parent's response mesh with the child's behavior?*
- *Did the parent ignore the child?*
- *Did the parent allow the child to self-initiate?*
- *Does it appear that the family's culture influenced interactions between the parent and child and the child's use of his or her systems?*

*Let's use the Developmental Characteristics Chart to compare the child's task performance with that of other children in the same age range. What do we learn from the comparisons?*

# REFLECTIVE PARENT INTERVIEW FOR THE FIRST VISIT

**SUPERVISOR TO THE DIRECT CARE PRACTITIONER:**

*What seemed most important in the parent's responses to the questions? We will write these replies in the child's record. Did the parent interact with the child during the interview? If so, we will need to describe these interactions in the child's record as well.*

| Interview area | Question(s) | Notes and observations |
|---|---|---|
| Family beginnings | How did you begin as a family? | |
| Role as a parent | How did you feel when you found out you were going to be a parent? Did you plan to have _____? | |
| Pregnancy and delivery | How did the pregnancy go? What was the delivery like? | |
| Family supports | What was it like for you when you first came home with _____? | |
| Parent's understanding of the child's cues | How does _____ tell you that he or she is hungry or tired? Please describe or mimic _____'s cries or signals regarding hunger or sleep. | |
| Separation | Have you and _____ ever been separated? Who else cared for (or cares for, if ongoing) your child? When? How did (or do) you feel about this? | |
| Intergenerational issues, culture, and values | Are you raising _____ in the same way that you were raised or in a different way? Do you follow your parents' customs? What languages do you speak at home? | |
| Caregiving needs | What are _____'s special needs? | |

*The Visit: Observation, Reflection, Synthesis for Training and Relationship Building,* by Annette Axtmann and Annegret Dettwiler.

**4–7 MONTHS**

# REFLECTIVE PARENT INTERVIEW FOR SUBSEQUENT VISITS

## SUPERVISOR TO THE DIRECT CARE PRACTITIONER:

*What seemed most important in the parent's responses to the questions? We will write these replies in the child's record. Did the parent interact with the child during the interview? If so, we will need to describe these interactions in the child's chart as well.*

| Interview area | Question(s) | Notes and observations |
|---|---|---|
| Family relationships | How are things going at home? | |
| Role as a parent | How do you feel now that you have been a parent for a while? | |
| Child's ongoing health and development | Do you have any new concerns about _____'s health or development? | |
| Family supports | Is your family supporting you? If so, how? | |
| Parent's understanding of the child's cues | Have you noticed any changes in the way that _____ lets you know what he or she wants or needs? Have you made any changes in the way that you are responding to _____? | |
| Relationship with the child care program | How has _____ been responding to the way that we are working with him or her? Have you felt included? | |
| Intergenerational issues, culture, and values | What kinds of things are you and _____ doing together at home? Are you raising _____ in the same way that you were raised or in a different way? | |
| Caregiving needs | Does _____ have any special needs at this time? | |

# SYNTHESIS

*We will now synthesize our observations from the meeting with the information gained during the reflective parent interview to address four areas in the spaces that follow. The answers to these questions, illustrated by our concrete observations, structure the letter for the parent.*

1. How did the child demonstrate strengths in his or her responses to the tasks, to the parent, and to us? How did the child coordinate his or her systems, and did the child initiate without prompting from the parent or supervisor?

2. How were these behaviors related to the interactions that we observed between the parent and child? How did the child contribute to these interactions?

---

3.  Does the parent have any special concerns? How did we agree with the parent to respond to these concerns?

4.  Are we concerned about the child's development in any way? If so, how can we suggest working with the family to strengthen the child's development within his or her social-cultural community?

# CLOSURE

## SUPERVISOR TO THE DIRECT CARE PRACTITIONER:

*How do you feel about working with this family?*

*I will transform our notes into the letter for the parent. Once you read and approve the letter, I'll ask you to sign it as well. Please let me know what you continue to observe on a daily basis. We will meet again to reflect together on this family and what we have learned about the family today, as well as what you are observing on a daily basis.*

*The Visit: Observation, Reflection, Synthesis for Training and Relationship Building,* by Annette Axtmann and Annegret Dettwiler.

NAME OF PRACTITIONER: _____

DATE OF VISIT: _____

NUMBER OF VISIT FOR PRACTITIONER: _____

CHILD'S AND PARENT'S NAMES: _____

_____

_____

The following sections detail the direct care practitioner's areas of strength and areas for future observation and follow-up.

## DURING THE MEETING

Observe the child and parent before interacting with them; this will allow your behavior to be tuned to the child and parent.

| Areas of strength | Areas for future observation and follow-up |
|---|---|
|  |  |

## DURING THE CO-REVIEW

Reflect before answering questions posed by the supervisor and illustrate answers (in part) with nonevaluative observations.

| Areas of strength | Areas for future observation and follow-up |
|---|---|
|  |  |

Describe systems used and/or systems not used by the child during tasks and during self-initiated behavior.

| Areas of strength | Areas for future observation and follow-up |
|---|---|
|  |  |

Relate observations to the child's history as told by the parent during the reflective parent interview (or related by the supervisor) that contribute to the synthesis of information collected from child and parent during the meeting.

| Areas of strength | Areas for future observation and follow-up |
|---|---|
|  |  |

**4–7 MONTHS**

Suggest one or two ways—based on observations and synthesis—to work with the family.

| Areas of strength | Areas for future observation and follow-up |
|---|---|
|  |  |

Relate knowledge of the nonlinear dynamic systems perspective of child development and basic principles of development to aspects of the child's and/or parent's behavior.

| Areas of strength | Areas for future observation and follow-up |
|---|---|
|  |  |

*The Visit: Observation, Reflection, Synthesis for Training and Relationship Building*, by Annette Axtmann and Annegret Dettwiler.

## OBSERVATION, REFLECTION, SYNTHESIS GUIDE AND VISIT RECORD FOR

CHILD'S NAME: _____

CHILD'S DATE OF BIRTH: _____

DATE OF VISIT: _____

## AGE RANGE: 7–10 MONTHS

## FOR THE SUPERVISOR

The Visit is an opportunity for you to provide in-service training for caregivers, home visitors, social services coordinators, and family child care providers and for you to strengthen your work with families. These goals will be accomplished through

OBSERVATION    REFLECTION    SYNTHESIS

## PREPARE FOR THE MEETING:

- Review the child's medical record, enrollment form, and/or prior records from the Visit.
- Obtain a blank copy of the appropriate-age Guide by photocopying it from the book or printing it from the accompanying CD-ROM.
- Fill in the child's name throughout the Guide.
- Secure the materials needed for the tasks. These vary according to the child's age range; see the Meeting section of this Guide for the task-specific materials.
- Prioritize the interview questions according to which issues might be most important for the family.
- Consider how the direct care practitioner will be included throughout the meeting with the family.

## DURING THE MEETING:

- Observe interactions among the direct care practitioner, the child, the parent, and, if present, other family members. Be guided by your observations.
- Ask the parent to choose whether to begin with the reflective parent interview or tasks for the child.
- Observe parent–child interactions. Comment *in the moment* on beneficial interactions. Doing so will empower the parent and instruct the direct care practitioner.
- Observe which systems (social-emotional, visual, motor, cognitive, communication) the child uses to solve the task, and how the child solves the task.
- Observe which system(s) the child does not use to solve the task.
- Observe the child's self-initiated behavior and ask yourself how the child's behavior relates to parent–child interactions.
- Pause after each interview question to give the parent time to reflect.
- Do not take notes during the meeting. (Notes can be taken during the co-review.)

## DURING THE CO-REVIEW:

- Ask the direct care practitioner questions as listed in the co-review section of this Guide, and use his or her answers to guide the co-review.
- Share concrete observations, and reflect together on how they relate to
  - The parent–child relationship
  - The child's use of social-emotional, visual, motor, cognitive, and communication systems during tasks
  - The child's self-initiated behavior

---

**7–10 MONTHS**    2

- Use the Visit's Developmental Characteristics Chart to compare the child's behavior to that of others in his or her age range.

**SYNTHESIZE:**
- Synthesize the parent's responses during the reflective parent interview with observations made by the team during the meeting. Observations should include which systems the child used or did not use and the child's behavior as compared with others in his or her age range.
- Use the synthesis to write a letter for the parent. The letter should summarize what you and the direct care practitioner have learned and how you have agreed with the parent to work for the child's benefit. Illustrate the letter with observations made by you and the direct care practitioner.
- Fill out the Future Supervision for Direct Care Practitioner Form.

*Remember that how you act is as important as what you do.*

*The Visit: Observation, Reflection, Synthesis for Training and Relationship Building,* by Annette Axtmann and Annegret Dettwiler.

# MEETING
## AGE RANGE: 7–10 MONTHS

**MATERIALS:**

Red or multicolored rings, cubes, doll, cloth, Cheerios

**CREATE A SPACE (IN THE HOME OR CHILD CARE SETTING) TO ADMINISTER THE VISIT:**

Place a blanket on the floor near an object that the child can use to pull to stand. Clear a space on an adult-size table.

**SUPERVISOR TO THE DIRECT CARE PRACTITIONER:**

*You are here to exchange information with the family because you provide direct care for the child—meaning that the family considers you a very important person in the service system. There are two parts to our meeting with the family: 1) tasks for the child and 2) a reflective parent interview. During the interview, allow the child to explore and to interact with his or her parent naturally. Please allow the child to cry, crawl, or walk to establish contact with his or her parent. Do not pull the child back or ask the parent for help. We want to observe how the parent responds—or does not respond—to the child while he or she is answering sensitive questions. We need to observe how the parent and child interact because the child's growth and development depend on parent–child interactions.*

**SUPERVISOR TO THE PARENT:**

*Welcome. You were asked to participate in this meeting so that we can exchange infor-mation and share the care of your child with you. We will administer some develop-mental tasks to determine _____'s individual competencies. As you are part of _____'s family, we will ask you some questions about him or her. Please care for _____ or ask the direct care practitioner to do so when you feel it is best. We will observe how you interact with _____ so that we can perhaps imitate you while we are caring for him or her. This meeting takes approximately 30 minutes. Would you prefer to begin with the interview questions or the tasks?*

**OVERALL DIRECTIONS FOR THE SUPERVISOR DURING THE MEETING:**

- Remember that observations are nonevaluative; they will be interpreted and discussed during the co-review.
- Ask all participants to sit on the floor, at the child's eye level.
- Observe the child's eye contact, smiles, and vocalizations.
- Compare the child's reactions to the parent (as a familiar person) and to you (as a stranger).
- Observe and comment on the competence expressed by the child's self-initiated behaviors.

*The Visit: Observation, Reflection, Synthesis for Training and Relationship Building,* by Annette Axtmann and Annegret Dettwiler.

- Ask the parent to administer the tasks that are italicized in the chart, and do not interfere when the parent administers a task.
- If the child does not do a task, ask the parent if the child does it at home.

## WHAT TO LOOK FOR DURING PARENT–CHILD INTERACTIONS:
- Clarity of the child's behavior toward the parent (e.g., eye contact, vocalizations, body movement)
- Contingent parent responses to the child
- Noncontingent parent responses to the child
- No parent response to the child (i.e., parent ignores the child)
- Child self-initiated actions (i.e., whether the parent permits them)
- Cultural aspects of parent–child interactions

## TASKS
### GUIDELINES FOR ADMINISTERING AND OBSERVING PERFORMANCE OF THE TASKS

| Task and related systems | Cues for administration | Strengths and needs to observe as the child responds to the tasks |
|---|---|---|
| **Makes the transition to sitting**<br>Visual<br>Motor<br>Cognitive | *Ask the parent to place the child on his or her back.*<br>Observe the child's attempts to change position.<br>Shake the rings; hold or place them in an elevated position. | Coordination of visual and motor systems<br>Ability to obtain a vertical position |
| **Sits**<br>Visual<br>Motor<br>Cognitive | Observe the child's ability to maintain balance when reaching for the rings when they are placed out of reach. | Balance control in sitting<br>Symmetry of posture<br>Eye–hand coordination |
| **Crawls**<br>Visual<br>Motor<br>Cognitive | Encourage the child to move from a sitting into a crawling position by placing the rings out of reach.<br>Observe the child's crawling. | Mobility (on the floor)<br>Coordination of visual and motor systems |
| **Pulls to standing**<br>Visual<br>Motor<br>Cognitive | Place the rings or another small object on a small table.<br>Observe how the child pulls to stand.<br>Observe the child's steadiness in standing. | Coordination of visual and motor systems<br>Ability to obtain a vertical position<br>Balance control in standing |

*The Visit: Observation, Reflection, Synthesis for Training and Relationship Building*, by Annette Axtmann and Annegret Dettwiler.

| Task and related systems | Cues for administration | Strengths and needs to observe as the child responds to the tasks |
|---|---|---|
| **Manipulates the cubes**<br>Visual<br>Motor<br>Cognitive | *Ask the parent to sit at the table with the child on his or her lap so that the child is facing the table.*<br>Place one cube within the child's reach on the table or on the parent's palm.<br>Observe the type of grasp used and the child's ability to hold the cube in his or her right or left hand.<br>Place another cube on the table.<br>Observe whether the child bangs the two cubes together on the table.<br>Observe whether the child tracks the cube with his or her eyes if it falls on floor.<br>Encourage imitation by demonstration. | Eye–hand coordination<br>Shapes hand to object (adaptive)<br>Recognition of the relationship between inanimate objects<br>Imitation skills |
| **Uncovers the doll**<br>Cognitive<br>Visual<br>Social-emotional<br>Motor | Place the doll in a sitting position, then use the cloth to cover the doll while the child is looking.<br>Note the child's reaction and any attempt to uncover the doll or another object of greater interest.<br>You may cover your face with the cloth or *ask the parent to cover his or her face with the cloth.* | Object permanence |
| **Feeds self**<br>Visual<br>Motor | *Ask the parent to place Cheerios in front of the child.*<br>Observe the child's grasp.<br>Observe whether the child brings the food to his or her mouth. | Adaptation of grasp<br>Coordination of visual and motor systems<br>Eye–hand coordination (adaptive)<br>Self-regulation |
| **Vocalizes "mama" and "dada"**<br>Communication | Observe spontaneous vocalizations such as "mama" or "dada."<br>*Ask the parent what vocalizations the child typically makes at home.* | Production of sounds<br>Expression of affect |

**7–10 MONTHS**  6

*The Visit: Observation, Reflection, Synthesis for Training and Relationship Building,* by Annette Axtmann and Annegret Dettwiler.
© 2005 Paul H. Brookes Publishing Co. All rights reserved.

# REFLECTIVE PARENT INTERVIEW

## QUESTIONS FOR THE FIRST VISIT

Please use the following script as a guide only. Prioritize the order of the questions according to what you already know and are learning about the child and parent during this meeting with them. Wait for the parent to reflect and to respond fully—in whatever way seems comfortable for him or her. Remember that some questions can be left for later during the family's participation in the program. As you ask questions, observe how the parent maintains a balance between responding to the questions and to the demands made by the child. **Do not take notes.**

| INTERVIEW AREA | QUESTION(S) |
|---|---|
| Family beginnings | *How did you begin as a family?* |
| Role as a parent | *How did you feel when you found out you were going to be a parent? Did you plan to have _____?* |
| Pregnancy and delivery | *How did the pregnancy go? What was the delivery like?* |
| Family supports | *What was it like for you when you first came home with _____?* |
| Parent's understanding of the child's cues | *How does _____ tell you that he or she is hungry or tired? Please describe or mimic _____'s cries or signals regarding hunger or sleep.* |
| Separation | *Have you and _____ ever been separated? Who else has cared for (or cares for, if ongoing) your child? When? How did (or do) you feel about this?* |
| Intergenerational issues, culture, and values | *Are you raising _____ in the same way that you were raised or in a different way? Do you follow your parents' customs? What languages do you speak at home?* |
| Caregiving needs | *What are _____'s special needs?* |

## CLOSURE OF THE MEETING

*There is much more for us to learn from one another. We will write you a letter summarizing what we have learned about _____ and how we all have agreed to work with him (or her). We appreciate the time that you and _____ have spent with us. Thank you.*

# REFLECTIVE PARENT INTERVIEW

## QUESTIONS FOR SUBSEQUENT VISITS

Please use the following script as a guide only. Prioritize the order of the questions according to what you already know and are learning about the child and parent during this meeting with them. Wait for the parent to reflect and to respond fully—in whatever way seems comfortable for him or her. Remember that some questions can be left for later during the family's participation in the program. As you ask questions, observe how the parent maintains a balance between responding to the questions and to the demands made by the child. **Do not take notes.**

| INTERVIEW AREA | QUESTION(S) |
|---|---|
| Family relationships | *How are things going at home?* |
| Role as a parent | *How do you feel now that you have been a parent for a while?* |
| Child's ongoing health and development | *Do you have any new concerns about _____'s health or development?* |
| Family supports | *Is your family supporting you? If so, how?* |
| Parent's understanding of the child's cues | *Have you noticed any changes in the way that _____ lets you know what he or she wants or needs? Have you made any changes in the way that you are responding to _____?* |
| Relationship with the program | *How has _____ been responding to the way that we are working with him or her? Have you felt included?* |
| Intergenerational issues, culture, and values | *What kinds of things are you and _____ doing together at home? Are you raising _____ in the same way that you were raised or in a different way?* |
| Caregiving needs | *Does _____ have any special needs at this time?* |

## CLOSURE OF THE MEETING

*There is much more for us to learn from one another. We will write you a letter summarizing what we have learned about _____ and how we all have agreed to work with him (or her). We appreciate the time that you and _____ have spent with us. Thank you.*

## CO-REVIEW OF VISIT # _____
## FOR CHILD'S ONGOING RECORD

CHILD'S NAME: _____

DATE OF VISIT: _____

CHILD'S AGE AT TIME OF VISIT (IN MONTHS AND DAYS): _____

TEAM MEMBERS: SUPERVISOR _____

DIRECT CARE PRACTITIONER _____

NAME(S) OF CHILD'S FAMILY MEMBER(S) IN ATTENDANCE: _____

_____

_____

HEALTH ISSUES NOTED ON CHILD'S MEDICAL FORM: _____

_____

_____

**MATERIALS:**
Pencil, Developmental Characteristics Chart

**SUPERVISOR INTRODUCES THE CO-REVIEW TO THE DIRECT CARE PRACTITIONER:**

*During this co-review, we will share our observations of the child and his or her parent. We will relate these observations to what each of us remembers about the child's response to his or her parent and to us, the child's self-initiated behaviors, the child's performance of the tasks, and the parent's answers during the interview. In addition, we will record observations of parent–child interactions in the right-hand column of the chart that follows. Overall, we will ask the following questions during this co-review:*

- *What do the observations indicate about the child's strengths and/or needs? How were these areas of strength or need influenced by the child's interactions with his or her parent?*
- *Which systems did the child use or not use to solve the tasks?*
- *Did the child's behavior during the meeting indicate that the child's systems are in balance or off balance?*

*As we synthesize this information, we will develop a picture of the child within the context of his or her family. We will use this picture to draft a letter to the parent summarizing what we and the parent agreed to do for the child's well-being. We will illustrate the letter with our observations.*

## CHILD'S STRENGTHS AND NEEDS

**SUPERVISOR TO THE DIRECT CARE PRACTITIONER:**

*We will share our observations of how the child used his or her various systems to solve each task. This will enable us to uncover the child's strengths. If the parent reported that he or she has seen the child do the task at home, we will note that here as well.*

*The Visit: Observation, Reflection, Synthesis for Training and Relationship Building,* by Annette Axtmann and Annegret Dettwiler.

| Task and related systems | Observations of how the child used his or her systems | Observations of parent–child interactions during the task |
|---|---|---|
| **Makes the transition to sitting**<br>Visual<br>Motor<br>Cognitive | Did the child sit up?<br>Did the child move to another position? | |
| **Sits**<br>Visual<br>Motor<br>Cognitive | Did the child sit steadily and independently?<br>Was the child's posture symmetrical?<br>Did the child reach out and grasp the rings? | |
| **Crawls**<br>Visual<br>Motor<br>Cognitive | Did the child move from a sitting position into a crawling position?<br>Did the child crawl using an alternating pattern? | |
| **Pulls to standing**<br>Visual<br>Motor<br>Cognitive | Did the child pull to a standing position while holding on to a small table?<br>Did the child stand steadily while holding on to the small table?<br>Was the child's posture symmetrical? | |
| **Manipulates the cubes**<br>Visual<br>Motor<br>Cognitive | Did the child grasp the cube?<br>Which type of grasp did the child use?<br>Did the child bang the two cubes together at his or her own initiative or after demonstration? | |
| **Uncovers the doll**<br>Cognitive<br>Visual<br>Social-emotional<br>Motor | Did the child uncover the doll at his or her own initiative and purposefully?<br>Did the child uncover the doll after demonstration?<br>Did the child vocalize or demonstrate facial affect? | |
| **Feeds self**<br>Visual<br>Motor | Which type of grasp did the child use to pick up any Cheerios?<br>Did the child bring the Cheerios to his or her mouth to eat? | |
| **Vocalizes "mama" and "dada"**<br>Communication | Did the child vocalize at his or her own initiative?<br>Did the child imitate your vocalizations or those of the parent? | |

*The Visit: Observation, Reflection, Synthesis for Training and Relationship Building*, by Annette Axtmann and Annegret Dettwiler.

- *What are the child's strengths, and how do they seem to relate to our observations of parent–child interactions?*
- *Did the parent and child interact during the tasks, and did these interactions influence the child's performance of the tasks?*
- *Did the parent seem to understand the child's behavior?*
- *Did the parent's response mesh with the child's behavior?*
- *Did the parent ignore the child?*
- *Did the parent allow the child to self-initiate?*
- *Does it appear that the family's culture influenced interactions between the parent and child and the child's use of his or her systems?*

*Let's use the Developmental Characteristics Chart to compare the child's task performance with that of other children in the same age range. What do we learn from the comparisons?*

*The Visit: Observation, Reflection, Synthesis for Training and Relationship Building,* by Annette Axtmann and Annegret Dettwiler.

# REFLECTIVE PARENT INTERVIEW FOR THE FIRST VISIT

## SUPERVISOR TO THE DIRECT CARE PRACTITIONER:

*What seemed most important in the parent's responses to the questions? We will write these replies in the child's record. Did the parent interact with the child during the interview? If so, we will need to describe these interactions in the child's record as well.*

| Interview area | Question(s) | Notes and observations |
|---|---|---|
| Family beginnings | How did you begin as a family? | |
| Role as a parent | How did you feel when you found out you were going to be a parent? Did you plan to have _____? | |
| Pregnancy and delivery | How did the pregnancy go? What was the delivery like? | |
| Family supports | What was it like for you when you first came home with _____? | |
| Parent's understanding of the child's cues | How does _____ tell you that he or she is hungry or tired? Please describe or mimic _____'s cries or signals regarding hunger or sleep. | |
| Separation | Have you and _____ ever been separated? Who else cared for (or cares for, if ongoing) your child? When? How did (or do) you feel about this? | |
| Intergenerational issues, culture, and values | Are you raising _____ in the same way that you were raised or in a different way? Do you follow your parents' customs? What languages do you speak at home? | |
| Caregiving needs | What are _____'s special needs? | |

*The Visit: Observation, Reflection, Synthesis for Training and Relationship Building*, by Annette Axtmann and Annegret Dettwiler.
© 2005 Paul H. Brookes Publishing Co. All rights reserved.

**7–10 MONTHS**

# REFLECTIVE PARENT INTERVIEW FOR SUBSEQUENT VISITS

## SUPERVISOR TO THE DIRECT CARE PRACTITIONER:

*What seemed most important in the parent's responses to the questions? We will write these replies in the child's record. Did the parent interact with the child during the interview? If so, we will need to describe these interactions in the child's chart as well.*

| Interview area | Question(s) | Notes and observations |
|---|---|---|
| Family relationships | How are things going at home? | |
| Role as a parent | How do you feel now that you have been a parent for a while? | |
| Child's ongoing health and development | Do you have any new concerns about _____'s health or development? | |
| Family supports | Is your family supporting you? If so, how? | |
| Parent's understanding of the child's cues | Have you noticed any changes in the way that _____ lets you know what he or she wants or needs? Have you made any changes in the way that you are responding to _____? | |
| Relationship with the child care program | How has _____ been responding to the way that we are working with him or her? Have you felt included? | |
| Intergenerational issues, culture, and values | What kinds of things are you and _____ doing together at home? Do you find that you are raising _____ in the same way that you were raised or in a different way? | |
| Caregiving needs | Does _____ have any special needs at this time? | |

*The Visit: Observation, Reflection, Synthesis for Training and Relationship Building,* by Annette Axtmann and Annegret Dettwiler.

# SYNTHESIS

**SUPERVISOR TO THE DIRECT CARE PRACTITIONER:**

*We will now synthesize our observations from the meeting with the information gained during the reflective parent interview to address four areas in the spaces that follow. The answers to these questions, illustrated by our concrete observations, structure the letter for the parent.*

1.  How did the child demonstrate strengths in his or her responses to the tasks, to the parent, and to us? How did the child coordinate his or her systems, and did the child initiate without prompting from the parent or supervisor?

2.  How were these behaviors related to the interactions that we observed between the parent and child? How did the child contribute to these interactions?

3.  Does the parent have any special concerns? How did we agree with the parent to respond to these concerns?

4.  Are we concerned about the child's development in any way? If so, how can we suggest working with the family to strengthen the child's development within his or her social-cultural community?

# CLOSURE

*How do you feel about working with this family?*

*I will transform our notes into the letter for the parent. Once you read and approve the letter, I'll ask you to sign it as well. Please let me know what you continue to observe on a daily basis. We will meet again to reflect together on this family and what we have learned about the family today, as well as what you are observing on a daily basis.*

## FUTURE SUPERVISION FOR DIRECT CARE PRACTITIONER FORM

NAME OF PRACTITIONER: _____

DATE OF VISIT: _____

NUMBER OF VISIT FOR PRACTITIONER: _____

CHILD'S AND PARENT'S NAMES: _____

_____

_____

The following sections detail the direct care practitioner's areas of strength and areas for future observation and follow-up.

### DURING THE MEETING
Observe the child and parent before interacting with them; this will allow your behavior to be tuned to the child and parent.

| Areas of strength | Areas for future observation and follow-up |
|---|---|
| | |

Reflect before answering questions posed by the supervisor and illustrate answers (in part) with nonevaluative observations.

| Areas of strength | Areas for future observation and follow-up |
|---|---|
|  |  |

Describe systems used and/or systems not used by the child during tasks and during self-initiated behavior.

| Areas of strength | Areas for future observation and follow-up |
|---|---|
|  |  |

Relate observations to the child's history as told by the parent during the reflective parent interview (or related by the supervisor) that contribute to the synthesis of information collected from child and parent during the meeting.

| Areas of strength | Areas for future observation and follow-up |
|---|---|
|  |  |

Suggest one or two ways—based on observations and synthesis—to work with the family.

| Areas of strength | Areas for future observation and follow-up |
|---|---|
| | |

Relate knowledge of the nonlinear dynamic systems perspective of child development and basic principles of development to aspects of the child's and/or parent's behavior.

| Areas of strength | Areas for future observation and follow-up |
|---|---|
| | |

## OBSERVATION, REFLECTION, SYNTHESIS GUIDE AND VISIT RECORD FOR

CHILD'S NAME: _____

CHILD'S DATE OF BIRTH: _____

DATE OF VISIT: _____

## AGE RANGE: 10–13 MONTHS

## For the supervisor

The Visit is an opportunity for you to provide in-service training for caregivers, home visitors, social services coordinators, and family child care providers and for you to strengthen your work with families. These goals will be accomplished through

OBSERVATION    REFLECTION    SYNTHESIS

## Prepare for the meeting:

- Review the child's medical record, enrollment form, and/or prior records from the Visit.
- Obtain a blank copy of the appropriate-age Guide by photocopying it from the book or printing it from the accompanying CD-ROM.
- Fill in the child's name throughout the Guide.
- Secure the materials needed for the tasks. These vary according to the child's age range; see the Meeting section of this Guide for the task-specific materials.
- Prioritize the interview questions according to which issues might be most important for the family.
- Consider how the direct care practitioner will be included throughout the meeting with the family.

## During the meeting:

- Observe interactions among the direct care practitioner, the child, the parent, and, if present, other family members. Be guided by your observations.
- Ask the parent to choose whether to begin with the reflective parent interview or tasks for the child.
- Observe parent–child interactions. Comment *in the moment* on beneficial interactions. Doing so will empower the parent and instruct the direct care practitioner.
- Observe which systems (social-emotional, visual, motor, cognitive, communication) the child uses to solve the task, and how the child solves the task.
- Observe which system(s) the child does not use to solve the task.
- Observe the child's self-initiated behavior and ask yourself how the child's behavior relates to parent–child interactions.
- Pause after each interview question to give the parent time to reflect.
- Do not take notes during the meeting. (Notes can be taken during the co-review.)

## During the co-review:

- Ask the direct care practitioner questions as listed in the co-review section of this Guide, and use his or her answers to guide the co-review.
- Share concrete observations, and reflect together on how they relate to
  - The parent–child relationship
  - The child's use of social-emotional, visual, motor, cognitive, and communication systems during tasks
  - The child's self-initiated behavior

- Use the Visit's Developmental Characteristics Chart to compare the child's behavior to that of others in his or her age range.

### SYNTHESIZE:

- Synthesize the parent's responses during the reflective parent interview with observations made by the team during the meeting. Observations should include which systems the child used or did not use and the child's behavior as compared with others in his or her age range.
- Use the synthesis to write a letter for the parent. The letter should summarize what you and the direct care practitioner have learned and how you have agreed with the parent to work for the child's benefit. Illustrate the letter with observations made by you and the direct care practitioner.
- Fill out the Future Supervision for Direct Care Practitioner Form.

*Remember that how you act is as important as what you do.*

# Meeting

## Age Range: 10–13 Months

**Materials:**

Red cubes, cup, Cheerios, crayon, paper, jar, cloth, red or multicolored rings

**Create a space (in the home or child care setting) to administer the Visit:**

Identify an object that the child can use to pull to stand. Clear a space on an adult-size table.

**Supervisor to the direct care practitioner:**

*You are here to exchange information with the family because you provide direct care for the child—meaning that the family considers you a very important person in the service system. There are two parts to our meeting with the family: 1) tasks for the child and 2) a reflective parent interview. During the interview, allow the child to explore and to interact with his or her parent naturally. Please allow the child to cry, crawl, or walk to establish contact with his or her parent. Do not pull the child back or ask the parent for help. We want to observe how the parent responds—or does not respond—to the child while he or she is answering sensitive questions. We need to observe how the parent and child interact because the child's growth and development depend on parent–child interactions.*

**Supervisor to the parent:**

*Welcome. You were asked to participate in this meeting so that we can exchange information and share the care of your child with you. We will administer some developmental tasks to determine _____'s individual competencies. As you are part of _____'s family, we will ask you some questions about him or her. Please care for _____ or ask the direct care practitioner to do so when you feel it is best. We will observe how you interact with _____ so that we can perhaps imitate you while we are caring for him or her. This meeting takes approximately 30 minutes. Would you prefer to begin with the interview questions or the tasks?*

**Overall directions for the supervisor during the meeting:**

- Remember that observations are nonevaluative; they will be interpreted and discussed during the co-review.
- Ask all participants to sit on the floor, at the child's eye level.
- Observe the child's eye contact, smiles, and vocalizations.
- Compare the child's reactions to the parent (as a familiar person) and to you (as a stranger).
- Observe and comment on the competence expressed by the child's self-initiated behaviors.
- Ask the parent to administer the tasks that are italicized in the chart, and do not interfere when the parent administers a task.
- If the child does not do a task, ask the parent if the child does it at home.

*The Visit: Observation, Reflection, Synthesis for Training and Relationship Building,* by Annette Axtmann and Annegret Dettwiler.

## What to look for during parent–child interactions:

- Clarity of the child's behavior toward the parent (e.g., eye contact, vocalizations, body movement)
- Contingent parent responses to the child
- Noncontingent parent responses to the child
- No parent response to the child (i.e., parent ignores the child)
- Child self-initiated actions (i.e., whether the parent permits them)
- Cultural aspects of parent–child interactions

## Tasks

### Guidelines for administering and observing performance of the tasks

| Task and related systems | Cues for administration | Strengths and needs to observe as the child responds to the tasks |
|---|---|---|
| **Stands and walks**<br>Cognitive<br>Motor<br>Visual | *Ask the parent to place the child in a sitting position near the object (e.g., small table, sofa) chosen for the child to use to pull to stand.*<br>Use the rings or other interesting objects on an elevated surface to encourage the child to pull to stand.<br>Observe the child as he or she pulls to stand, cruises, or walks without support. | Mobility<br>Coordination of visual and motor systems |
| **Manipulates a cube and the cup**<br>Cognitive<br>Visual<br>Motor | *Ask the parent to sit at the table with the child on his or her lap so that the child is facing the table.*<br>Place the cup and a cube in front of the child.<br>Observe the child's grasp and release of the cube into the cup.<br>Encourage the child by demonstration if necessary.<br>Hide the cube under the cup while the child is looking.<br>Observe the child's reaction and attempt to uncover the cube. | Coordination of visual and motor systems<br>Release function<br>Object permanence |

*The Visit: Observation, Reflection, Synthesis for Training and Relationship Building,* by Annette Axtmann and Annegret Dettwiler.

**10–13 MONTHS**

| Task and related systems | Cues for administration | Strengths and needs to observe as the child responds to the tasks |
|---|---|---|
| **Retrieves Cheerios**<br>Motor<br>Cognitive<br>Visual | *Ask the parent to place Cheerios in front of the child.*<br>Observe the child's grasp.<br>Observe whether the child brings Cheerios to his or her mouth.<br>Place a few Cheerios in the jar while the child is looking.<br>Offer the jar to the child, and observe the child's attempts to retrieve the Cheerios. | Adaptation of grasp<br>Coordination of visual and motor systems<br>Self-regulation (adaptive)<br>Relationship between objects |
| **Imitates scribbling**<br>Motor<br>Cognitive<br>Visual | Scribble on a piece of paper.<br>Offer the crayon to the child.<br>Observe the child's adaptation of grasp.<br>Ask the child to imitate your scribbling. | Coordination of visual and motor systems<br>Adaptation of grasp<br>Imitation skills |
| **Vocalizes words**<br>Communication<br>Cognitive<br>Visual<br>Motor | Observe any attempts at communication, noting gestures, vocalizations, and recognizable words.<br>*Ask for a parent report.* | Production of speech<br>Expression of affect |
| **Plays social games**<br>Communication<br>Social-emotional | *Ask the parent to play a social game with his or her child.*<br>Observe the child's participation. | Coordination of visual and motor systems during social interaction |

# REFLECTIVE PARENT INTERVIEW

## QUESTIONS FOR THE FIRST VISIT

Please use the following script as a guide only. Prioritize the order of the questions according to what you already know and are learning about the child and parent during this meeting with them. Wait for the parent to reflect and to respond fully—in whatever way seems comfortable for him or her. Remember that some questions can be left for later during the family's participation in the program. As you ask questions, observe how the parent maintains a balance between responding to the questions and to the demands made by the child. **Do not take notes.**

| INTERVIEW AREA | QUESTION(S) |
|---|---|
| Family beginnings | *How did you begin as a family?* |
| Role as a parent | *How did you feel when you found out you were going to be a parent? Did you plan to have _____?* |
| Pregnancy and delivery | *How did the pregnancy go? What was the delivery like?* |
| Family supports | *What was it like for you when you first came home with _____?* |
| Parent's understanding of the child's cues | *How does _____ tell you that he or she is hungry or tired? Please describe or mimic _____'s cries or signals regarding hunger or sleep.* |
| Separation | *Have you and _____ ever been separated? Who else has cared for (or cares for, if ongoing) your child? When? How did (or do) you feel about this?* |
| Intergenerational issues, culture, and values | *Are you raising _____ in the same way that you were raised or in a different way? Do you follow your parents' customs? What languages do you speak at home?* |
| Caregiving needs | *What are _____'s special needs?* |

## CLOSURE OF THE MEETING

*There is much more for us to learn from one another. We will write you a letter summarizing what we have learned about _____ and how we all have agreed to work with him (or her). We appreciate the time that you and _____ have spent with us. Thank you.*

# REFLECTIVE PARENT INTERVIEW

## QUESTIONS FOR SUBSEQUENT VISITS

Please use the following script as a guide only. Prioritize the order of the questions according to what you already know and are learning about the child and parent during this meeting with them. Wait for the parent to reflect and to respond fully—in whatever way seems comfortable for him or her. Remember that some questions can be left for later during the family's participation in the program. As you ask questions, observe how the parent maintains a balance between responding to the questions and to the demands made by the child. **Do not take notes.**

| INTERVIEW AREA | QUESTION(S) |
|---|---|
| Family relationships | *How are things going at home?* |
| Role as a parent | *How do you feel now that you have been a parent for a while?* |
| Child's ongoing health and development | *Do you have any new concerns about _____'s health or development?* |
| Family supports | *Is your family supporting you? If so, how?* |
| Parent's understanding of the child's cues | *Have you noticed any changes in the way that _____ lets you know what he or she wants or needs? Have you made any changes in the way that you are responding to _____?* |
| Relationship with the program | *How has _____ been responding to the way that we are working with him or her? Have you felt included?* |
| Intergenerational issues, culture, and values | *What kinds of things are you and _____ doing together at home? Are you raising _____ in the same way that you were raised or in a different way?* |
| Caregiving needs | *Does _____ have any special needs at this time?* |

## CLOSURE OF THE MEETING

*There is much more for us to learn from one another. We will write you a letter summarizing what we have learned about _____ and how we all have agreed to work with him (or her). We appreciate the time that you and _____ have spent with us. Thank you.*

CHILD'S NAME: _____

DATE OF VISIT: _____

CHILD'S AGE AT TIME OF VISIT (IN MONTHS AND DAYS): _____

TEAM MEMBERS: SUPERVISOR _____

DIRECT CARE PRACTITIONER _____

NAME(S) OF CHILD'S FAMILY MEMBER(S) IN ATTENDANCE: _____

_____

_____

HEALTH ISSUES NOTED ON CHILD'S MEDICAL FORM: _____

_____

_____

**MATERIALS:**
Pencil, Developmental Characteristics Chart

**SUPERVISOR INTRODUCES THE CO-REVIEW TO THE DIRECT CARE PRACTITIONER:**

*During this co-review, we will share our observations of the child and his or her parent. We will relate these observations to what each of us remembers about the child's response to his or her parent and to us, the child's self-initiated behaviors, the child's performance of the tasks, and the parent's answers during the interview. In addition, we will record observations of parent–child interactions in the right-hand column of the chart that follows. Overall, we will ask the following questions during this co-review:*

- *What do the observations indicate about the child's strengths and/or needs? How were these areas of strength or need influenced by the child's interactions with his or her parent?*
- *Which systems did the child use or not use to solve the tasks?*
- *Did the child's behavior during the meeting indicate that the child's systems are in balance or off balance?*

*As we synthesize this information, we will develop a picture of the child within the context of his or her family. We will use this picture to draft a letter to the parent summarizing what we and the parent agreed to do for the child's well-being. We will illustrate the letter with our observations.*

## CHILD'S STRENGTHS AND NEEDS

**SUPERVISOR TO THE DIRECT CARE PRACTITIONER:**

*We will share our observations of how the child used his or her various systems to solve each task. This will enable us to uncover the child's strengths. If the parent reported that he or she has seen the child do the task at home, we will note that here as well.*

*The Visit: Observation, Reflection, Synthesis for Training and Relationship Building,* by Annette Axtmann and Annegret Dettwiler.
© 2005 Paul H. Brookes Publishing Co. All rights reserved.

| Task and related systems | Observations of how the child used his or her systems | Observations of parent–child interactions during the task |
|---|---|---|
| **Stands and walks**<br>Motor<br>Cognitive<br>Visual | Did the child pull to a standing position while holding on to a piece of furniture?<br>Was the child able to stand steadily when holding on to a table?<br>Was the child able to stand steadily without support?<br>Did the child cruise?<br>Did the child walk without support? | |
| **Manipulates a cube and the cup**<br>Cognitive<br>Visual<br>Motor | Did the child release the cube into the cup?<br>Did the child uncover the cube spontaneously?<br>Did the child uncover the cube after imitation?<br>Which type of grasp did the child use? | |
| **Retrieves Cheerios**<br>Motor<br>Cognitive<br>Visual | How did the child grasp a Cheerio?<br>Did the child bring the Cheerio to his or her mouth to eat?<br>Did the child dump the Cheerios from the jar? | |
| **Imitates scribbling**<br>Motor<br>Cognitive<br>Visual | How did the child grasp the crayon?<br>Did the child scribble with the crayon after demonstration? | |
| **Vocalizes words**<br>Communication<br>Cognitive<br>Visual<br>Motor | Did the child attempt to communicate with gestures?<br>Did the child vocalize at his or her own initiative?<br>Did the child produce recognizable words? | |
| **Plays social games**<br>Communication<br>Social-emotional | Did the child play a social game with his or her parent?<br>How did the child participate? | |

**10–13 MONTHS**

*The Visit: Observation, Reflection, Synthesis for Training and Relationship Building*, by Annette Axtmann and Annegret Dettwiler.

## Supervisor to the direct care practitioner:

- *What are the child's strengths, and how do they seem to relate to our observations of parent–child interactions?*
- *Did the parent and child interact during the tasks, and did these interactions influence the child's performance of the tasks?*
- *Did the parent seem to understand the child's behavior?*
- *Did the parent's response mesh with the child's behavior?*
- *Did the parent ignore the child?*
- *Did the parent allow the child to self-initiate?*
- *Does it appear that the family's culture influenced interactions between the parent and child and the child's use of his or her systems?*

*Let's use the Developmental Characteristics Chart to compare the child's task performance with that of other children in the same age range. What do we learn from the comparisons?*

*The Visit: Observation, Reflection, Synthesis for Training and Relationship Building*, by Annette Axtmann and Annegret Dettwiler.

# REFLECTIVE PARENT INTERVIEW FOR THE FIRST VISIT

**SUPERVISOR TO THE DIRECT CARE PRACTITIONER:**

*What seemed most important in the parent's responses to the questions? We will write these replies in the child's record. Did the parent interact with the child during the interview? If so, we will need to describe these interactions in the child's record as well.*

| Interview area | Question(s) | Notes and observations |
|---|---|---|
| Family beginnings | How did you begin as a family? | |
| Role as a parent | How did you feel when you found out you were going to be a parent? Did you plan to have _____? | |
| Pregnancy and delivery | How did the pregnancy go? What was the delivery like? | |
| Family supports | What was it like for you when you first came home with _____? | |
| Parent's understanding of the child's cues | How does _____ tell you that he or she is hungry or tired? Please describe or mimic _____'s cries or signals regarding hunger or sleep. | |
| Separation | Have you and _____ ever been separated? Who else cared for (or cares for, if ongoing) your child? When? How did (or do) you feel about this? | |
| Intergenerational issues, culture, and values | Are you raising _____ in the same way that you were raised or in a different way? Do you follow your parents' customs? What languages do you speak at home? | |
| Caregiving needs | What are _____'s special needs? | |

*The Visit: Observation, Reflection, Synthesis for Training and Relationship Building,* by Annette Axtmann and Annegret Dettwiler.
© 2005 Paul H. Brookes Publishing Co. All rights reserved.

**10–13 MONTHS**

# REFLECTIVE PARENT INTERVIEW FOR SUBSEQUENT VISITS

## SUPERVISOR TO THE DIRECT CARE PRACTITIONER:

*What seemed most important in the parent's responses to the questions? We will write these replies in the child's record. Did the parent interact with the child during the interview? If so, we will need to describe these interactions in the child's chart as well.*

| Interview area | Question(s) | Notes and observations |
|---|---|---|
| Family relationships | How are things going at home? | |
| Role as a parent | How do you feel now that you have been a parent for a while? | |
| Child's ongoing health and development | Do you have any new concerns about _____'s health or development? | |
| Family supports | Is your family supporting you? If so, how? | |
| Parent's understanding of the child's cues | Have you noticed any changes in the way that _____ lets you know what he or she wants or needs? Have you made any changes in the way that you are responding to _____? | |
| Relationship with the child care program | How has _____ been responding to the way that we are working with him or her? Have you felt included? | |
| Intergenerational issues, culture, and values | What kinds of things are you and _____ doing together at home? Are you raising _____ in the same way that you were raised or in a different way? | |
| Caregiving needs | Does _____ have any special needs at this time? | |

# SYNTHESIS

*We will now synthesize our observations from the meeting with the information gained during the reflective parent interview to address four areas in the spaces that follow. The answers to these questions, illustrated by our concrete observations, structure the letter for the parent.*

1. How did the child demonstrate strengths in his or her responses to the tasks, to the parent, and to us? How did the child coordinate his or her systems, and did the child initiate without prompting from the parent or supervisor?

2. How were these behaviors related to the interactions that we observed between the parent and child? How did the child contribute to these interactions?

---

3. Does the parent have any special concerns? How did we agree with the parent to respond to these concerns?

4. Are we concerned about the child's development in any way? If so, how can we suggest working with the family to strengthen the child's development within his or her social-cultural community?

*The Visit: Observation, Reflection, Synthesis for Training and Relationship Building*, by Annette Axtmann and Annegret Dettwiler.

## CLOSURE

**SUPERVISOR TO THE DIRECT CARE PRACTITIONER:**

*How do you feel about working with this family?*

*I will transform our notes into the letter for the parent. Once you read and approve the letter, I'll ask you to sign it as well. Please let me know what you continue to observe on a daily basis. We will meet again to reflect together on this family and what we have learned about the family today, as well as what you are observing on a daily basis.*

## FUTURE SUPERVISION
## FOR DIRECT CARE
## PRACTITIONER FORM

NAME OF PRACTITIONER: _____

DATE OF VISIT: _____

NUMBER OF VISIT FOR PRACTITIONER: _____

CHILD'S AND PARENT'S NAMES: _____

_____

_____

The following sections detail the direct care practitioner's areas of strength and areas for future observation and follow-up.

### DURING THE MEETING

Observe the child and parent before interacting with them; this will allow your behavior to be tuned to the child and parent.

| Areas of strength | Areas for future observation and follow-up |
|---|---|
|  |  |

*The Visit: Observation, Reflection, Synthesis for Training and Relationship Building*, by Annette Axtmann and Annegret Dettwiler.

Reflect before answering questions posed by the supervisor and illustrate answers (in part) with nonevaluative observations.

| Areas of strength | Areas for future observation and follow-up |
|---|---|
|  |  |

Describe systems used and/or systems not used by the child during tasks and during self-initiated behavior.

| Areas of strength | Areas for future observation and follow-up |
|---|---|
|  |  |

Relate observations to the child's history as told by the parent during the reflective parent interview (or related by the supervisor) that contribute to the synthesis of information collected from child and parent during the meeting.

| Areas of strength | Areas for future observation and follow-up |
|---|---|
|  |  |

Suggest one or two ways—based on observations and synthesis—to work with the family.

| Areas of strength | Areas for future observation and follow-up |
|---|---|
| | |

Relate knowledge of the nonlinear dynamic systems perspective of child development and basic principles of development to aspects of the child's and/or parent's behavior.

| Areas of strength | Areas for future observation and follow-up |
|---|---|
| | |

# OBSERVATION, REFLECTION, SYNTHESIS GUIDE AND VISIT RECORD FOR

CHILD'S NAME: _____

CHILD'S DATE OF BIRTH: _____

DATE OF VISIT: _____

## AGE RANGE: 13–18 MONTHS

## For the supervisor

The Visit is an opportunity for you to provide in-service training for caregivers, home visitors, social services coordinators, and family child care providers and for you to strengthen your work with families. These goals will be accomplished through

OBSERVATION    REFLECTION    SYNTHESIS

## Prepare for the meeting:

- Review the child's medical record, enrollment form, and/or prior records from the Visit.
- Obtain a blank copy of the appropriate-age Guide by photocopying it from the book or printing it from the accompanying CD-ROM.
- Fill in the child's name throughout the Guide.
- Secure the materials needed for the tasks. These vary according to the child's age range; see the Meeting section of this Guide for the task-specific materials.
- Prioritize the interview questions according to which issues might be most important for the family.
- Consider how the direct care practitioner will be included throughout the meeting with the family.

## During the meeting:

- Observe interactions among the direct care practitioner, the child, the parent, and, if present, other family members. Be guided by your observations.
- Ask the parent to choose whether to begin with the reflective parent interview or tasks for the child.
- Observe parent–child interactions. Comment *in the moment* on beneficial interactions. Doing so will empower the parent and instruct the direct care practitioner.
- Observe which systems (social-emotional, visual, motor, cognitive, communication) the child uses to solve the task, and how the child solves the task.
- Observe which system(s) the child does not use to solve the task.
- Observe the child's self-initiated behavior and ask yourself how the child's behavior relates to parent–child interactions.
- Pause after each interview question to give the parent time to reflect.
- Do not take notes during the meeting. (Notes can be taken during the co-review.)

## During the co-review:

- Ask the direct care practitioner questions as listed in the co-review section of this Guide, and use his or her answers to guide the co-review.
- Share concrete observations, and reflect together on how they relate to
  - The parent–child relationship
  - The child's use of social-emotional, visual, motor, cognitive, and communication systems during tasks
  - The child's self-initiated behavior

---

- Use the Visit's Developmental Characteristics Chart to compare the child's behavior to that of others in his or her age range.

### SYNTHESIZE:
- Synthesize the parent's responses during the reflective parent interview with observations made by the team during the meeting. Observations should include which systems the child used or did not use and the child's behavior as compared with others in his or her age range.
- Use the synthesis to write a letter for the parent. The letter should summarize what you and the direct care practitioner have learned and how you have agreed with the parent to work for the child's benefit. Illustrate the letter with observations made by you and the direct care practitioner.
- Fill out the Future Supervision for Direct Care Practitioner Form.

*Remember that how you act is as important as what you do.*

# MEETING

## AGE RANGE: 13–18 MONTHS

**MATERIALS:**

Ball, red cubes, two cups, crayon, paper, Cheerios, jar, doll, spoon, bowl

**CREATE A SPACE (IN THE HOME OR CHILD CARE SETTING) TO ADMINISTER THE VISIT:**

Identify a space in which the child can move freely. Clear a space on an adult-size table.

**SUPERVISOR TO THE DIRECT CARE PRACTITIONER:**

*You are here to exchange information with the family because you provide direct care for the child—meaning that the family considers you a very important person in the service system. There are two parts to our meeting with the family: 1) tasks for the child and 2) a reflective parent interview. During the interview, allow the child to explore and to interact with his or her parent naturally. Please allow the child to cry, crawl, or walk to establish contact with his or her parent. Do not pull the child back or ask the parent for help. We want to observe how the parent responds—or does not respond—to the child while he or she is answering sensitive questions. We need to observe how the parent and child interact because the child's growth and development depend on parent–child interactions.*

**SUPERVISOR TO THE PARENT:**

*Welcome. You were asked to participate in this meeting so that we can exchange infor-mation and share the care of your child with you. We will administer some develop-mental tasks to determine _____'s individual competencies. As you are part of _____'s family, we will ask you some questions about him or her. Please care for _____ or ask the direct care practitioner to do so when you feel it is best. We will observe how you interact with _____ so that we can perhaps imitate you while we are caring for him or her. This meeting takes approximately 30 minutes. Would you prefer to begin with the interview questions or the tasks?*

**OVERALL DIRECTIONS FOR THE SUPERVISOR DURING THE MEETING:**

- Remember that observations are nonevaluative; they will be interpreted and discussed dur-ing the co-review.
- Ask all participants to sit on the floor, at the child's eye level.
- Observe the child's eye contact, smiles, and vocalizations.
- Compare the child's reactions to the parent (as a familiar person) and to you (as a stranger).
- Observe and comment on the competence expressed by the child's self-initiated behaviors.
- Ask the parent to administer the tasks that are italicized in the chart, and do not interfere when the parent administers a task.
- If the child does not do a task, ask the parent if the child does it at home.

---

　　　　　*The Visit: Observation, Reflection, Synthesis for Training and Relationship Building, by Annette Axtmann and Annegret Dettwiler.*

## WHAT TO LOOK FOR DURING PARENT–CHILD INTERACTIONS:

- Clarity of the child's behavior toward the parent (e.g., eye contact, vocalizations, body movement)
- Contingent parent responses to the child
- Noncontingent parent responses to the child
- No parent response to the child (i.e., parent ignores the child)
- Child self-initiated actions (i.e., whether the parent permits them)
- Cultural aspects of parent–child interactions

## TASKS

### GUIDELINES FOR ADMINISTERING AND OBSERVING PERFORMANCE OF THE TASKS

| Task and related systems | Cues for administration | Strengths and needs to observe as the child responds to the tasks |
|---|---|---|
| **Stands and walks**<br>Cognitive<br>Motor<br>Visual | Observe how the child stands.<br>Observe how the child cruises/walks.<br>Observe steadiness while standing and walking. | Mobility<br>Coordination of motor and visual systems |
| **Squats**<br>Motor<br>Visual | Place the ball on the floor.<br>Roll the ball toward the child.<br>Observe whether the child squats or bends down to touch the ball.<br>Observe the child's balance and steadiness. | Coordination of motor and visual systems |
| **Manipulates cubes**<br>Cognitive<br>Motor<br>Visual | *Ask the parent to help the child onto his or her lap or into a high chair at the table.*<br>Offer the child four to six cubes, one at a time.<br>Observe the child's grasp as he or she manipulates the cubes.<br>Observe whether the child stacks the cubes on his or her own initiative.<br>Demonstrate if the child does not stack the cubes on his or her own initiative.<br>Observe whether the child imitates. | Relationship between inanimate objects<br>Coordination of motor and visual systems<br>Imitation |

| Task and related systems | Cues for administration | Strengths and needs to observe as the child responds to the tasks |
|---|---|---|
| **Finds a cube under one of two cups**<br>Cognitive<br>Motor<br>Visual | Hide a cube under one of the two cups while the child is watching.<br>Ask the child to find the cube.<br>Hide the cube again, and reverse the position of the cups by sliding them past each other on the table.<br>Ask the child to find the cube.<br>Repeat this activity at least one more time to avoid accidental solutions on the child's part. | Object permanence<br>Coordination of motor and visual systems |
| **Imitates drawing a line**<br>Cognitive<br>Motor<br>Visual | Draw a single line on the piece of paper.<br>Offer the crayon to the child.<br>Observe whether the child imitates.<br>Observe the child's grasp of the crayon. | Coordination of visual and motor systems<br>Adaptation of grasp |
| **Places Cheerios in a jar**<br>Cognitive<br>Motor<br>Visual | Demonstrate dropping a Cheerio into the jar.<br>Offer the child six to eight Cheerios.<br>Observe the child's grasp as he or she imitates dropping Cheerios into the jar. | Adaptation of grasp<br>Coordination of visual and motor systems<br>Relationship between inanimate objects<br>Imitation |
| **Identifies familiar objects and/or body parts**<br>Communication<br>Cognitive<br>Visual<br>Motor | *Ask the parent to encourage the child to point to or name familiar objects in the environment.*<br>*Ask the parent to encourage the child to point to or name body parts on him- or herself or the doll.* | Coordination of visual, cognitive, and communication systems |
| **Feeds the doll or self with the spoon**<br>Social-emotional<br>Cognitive<br>Motor<br>Visual | *Ask the parent to offer the doll and spoon to the child.*<br>*Ask the parent to encourage the child to feed the doll or him- or herself.*<br>Observe the child's grasp of the spoon.<br>Observe whether the child engages in pretend play. | Coordination of actions with social-emotional, cognitive, and motor systems<br>Manipulation of spoon (adaptive) |

# Reflective Parent Interview

## Questions for the first Visit

Please use the following script as a guide only. Prioritize the order of the questions according to what you already know and are learning about the child and parent during this meeting with them. Wait for the parent to reflect and to respond fully—in whatever way seems comfortable for him or her. Remember that some questions can be left for later during the family's participation in the program. As you ask questions, observe how the parent maintains a balance between responding to the questions and to the demands made by the child. **Do not take notes.**

| Interview area | Question(s) |
| --- | --- |
| Family beginnings | *How did you begin as a family?* |
| Role as a parent | *How did you feel when you found out you were going to be a parent? Did you plan to have _____?* |
| Pregnancy and delivery | *How did the pregnancy go? What was the delivery like?* |
| Family supports | *What was it like for you when you first came home with _____?* |
| Parent's understanding of the child's cues | *How does _____ tell you that he or she is hungry or tired? Please describe or mimic _____'s cries or signals regarding hunger or sleep.* |
| Separation | *Have you and _____ ever been separated? Who else has cared for (or cares for, if ongoing) your child? When? How did (or do) you feel about this?* |
| Intergenerational issues, culture, and values | *Are you raising _____ in the same way that you were raised or in a different way? Do you follow your parents' customs? What languages do you speak at home?* |
| Caregiving needs | *What are _____'s special needs?* |

## Closure of the meeting

*There is much more for us to learn from one another. We will write you a letter summarizing what we have learned about _____ and how we all have agreed to work with him (or her). We appreciate the time that you and _____ have spent with us. Thank you.*

*The Visit: Observation, Reflection, Synthesis for Training and Relationship Building*, by Annette Axtmann and Annegret Dettwiler.
© 2005 Paul H. Brookes Publishing Co. All rights reserved.

**13–18 MONTHS**

# REFLECTIVE PARENT INTERVIEW

## QUESTIONS FOR SUBSEQUENT VISITS

Please use the following script as a guide only. Prioritize the order of the questions according to what you already know and are learning about the child and parent during this meeting with them. Wait for the parent to reflect and to respond fully—in whatever way seems comfortable for him or her. Remember that some questions can be left for later during the family's participation in the program. As you ask questions, observe how the parent maintains a balance between responding to the questions and to the demands made by the child. **Do not take notes.**

| INTERVIEW AREA | QUESTION(S) |
|---|---|
| Family relationships | *How are things going at home?* |
| Role as a parent | *How do you feel now that you have been a parent for a while?* |
| Child's ongoing health and development | *Do you have any new concerns about _____'s health or development?* |
| Family supports | *Is your family supporting you? If so, how?* |
| Parent's understanding of the child's cues | *Have you noticed any changes in the way that _____ lets you know what he or she wants or needs? Have you made any changes in the way that you are responding to _____?* |
| Relationship with the program | *How has _____ been responding to the way that we are working with him or her? Have you felt included?* |
| Intergenerational issues, culture, and values | *What kinds of things are you and _____ doing together at home? Are you raising _____ in the same way that you were raised or in a different way?* |
| Caregiving needs | *Does _____ have any special needs at this time?* |

## CLOSURE OF THE MEETING

*There is much more for us to learn from one another. We will write you a letter summarizing what we have learned about _____ and how we all have agreed to work with him (or her). We appreciate the time that you and _____ have spent with us. Thank you.*

CHILD'S NAME: _____

DATE OF VISIT: _____

CHILD'S AGE AT TIME OF VISIT (IN MONTHS AND DAYS): _____

TEAM MEMBERS: SUPERVISOR _____

DIRECT CARE PRACTITIONER _____

NAME(S) OF CHILD'S FAMILY MEMBER(S) IN ATTENDANCE: _____
_____
_____

HEALTH ISSUES NOTED ON CHILD'S MEDICAL FORM: _____
_____
_____

**MATERIALS:**
Pencil, Developmental Characteristics Chart

**SUPERVISOR INTRODUCES THE CO-REVIEW TO THE DIRECT CARE PRACTITIONER:**

*During this co-review, we will share our observations of the child and his or her parent. We will relate these observations to what each of us remembers about the child's response to his or her parent and to us, the child's self-initiated behaviors, the child's performance of the tasks, and the parent's answers during the interview. In addition, we will record observations of parent–child interactions in the right-hand column of the chart that follows. Overall, we will ask the following questions during this co-review:*

- *What do the observations indicate about the child's strengths and/or needs? How were these areas of strength or need influenced by the child's interactions with his or her parent?*
- *Which systems did the child use or not use to solve the tasks?*
- *Did the child's behavior during the meeting indicate that the child's systems are in balance or off balance?*

*As we synthesize this information, we will develop a picture of the child within the context of his or her family. We will use this picture to draft a letter to the parent summarizing what we and the parent agreed to do for the child's well-being. We will illustrate the letter with our observations.*

## CHILD'S STRENGTHS AND NEEDS

**SUPERVISOR TO THE DIRECT CARE PRACTITIONER:**

*We will share our observations of how the child used his or her various systems to solve each task. This will enable us to uncover the child's strengths. If the parent reported that he or she has seen the child do the task at home, we will note that here as well.*

*The Visit: Observation, Reflection, Synthesis for Training and Relationship Building*, by Annette Axtmann and Annegret Dettwiler.

| Task and related systems | Observations of how the child used his or her systems | Observations of parent–child interactions during the task |
|---|---|---|
| **Stands and walks**<br>Cognitive<br>Motor<br>Visual | Did the child stand without support?<br>Did the child walk without support?<br>Did the child stand and/or walk steadily? | |
| **Squats**<br>Motor<br>Visual | Did the child squat or bend down to touch the ball?<br>Was the child able to maintain his or her balance while squatting? | |
| **Manipulates cubes**<br>Cognitive<br>Motor<br>Visual | How did the child grasp a cube?<br>Did the child stack a tower of two to six cubes on his or her own initiative?<br>Did the child imitate stacking a tower? | |
| **Finds a cube under one of two cups**<br>Cognitive<br>Motor<br>Visual | Did the child find the cube under the cup?<br>Did the child find the cube under the cup when the cups were reversed? | |
| **Imitates drawing a line**<br>Cognitive<br>Motor<br>Visual | How did the child grasp the crayon?<br>Did the child imitate drawing a line on the piece of paper? | |
| **Places Cheerios in a jar**<br>Cognitive<br>Motor<br>Visual | How did the child grasp a Cheerio?<br>Did the child drop the Cheerios in the jar? | |
| **Identifies familiar objects and/or body parts**<br>Communication<br>Cognitive<br>Visual<br>Motor | Did the child point to a familiar object?<br>Did the child name a familiar object?<br>Did the child point to or name body parts on him- or herself or the doll? | |
| **Feeds the doll or self with the spoon**<br>Social-emotional<br>Cognitive<br>Motor<br>Visual | How did the child grasp the spoon?<br>Did the child engage in pretend play by feeding the doll or him- or herself? | |

**13–18 MONTHS**

**SUPERVISOR TO THE DIRECT CARE PRACTITIONER:**

- *What are the child's strengths, and how do they seem to relate to our observations of parent–child interactions?*
- *Did the parent and child interact during the tasks, and did these interactions influence the child's performance of the tasks?*
- *Did the parent seem to understand the child's behavior?*
- *Did the parent's response mesh with the child's behavior?*
- *Did the parent ignore the child?*
- *Did the parent allow the child to self-initiate?*
- *Does it appear that the family's culture influenced interactions between the parent and child and the child's use of his or her systems?*

*Let's use the Developmental Characteristics Chart to compare the child's task performance with that of other children in the same age range. What do we learn from the comparisons?*

# REFLECTIVE PARENT INTERVIEW FOR THE FIRST VISIT

## SUPERVISOR TO THE DIRECT CARE PRACTITIONER:

*What seemed most important in the parent's responses to the questions? We will write these replies in the child's record. Did the parent interact with the child during the interview? If so, we will need to describe these interactions in the child's record as well.*

| Interview area | Question(s) | Notes and observations |
|---|---|---|
| Family beginnings | How did you begin as a family? | |
| Role as a parent | How did you feel when you found out you were going to be a parent? Did you plan to have _____? | |
| Pregnancy and delivery | How did the pregnancy go? What was the delivery like? | |
| Family supports | What was it like for you when you first came home with _____? | |
| Parent's understanding of the child's cues | How does _____ tell you that he or she is hungry or tired? Please describe or mimic _____'s cries or signals regarding hunger or sleep. | |
| Separation | Have you and _____ ever been separated? Who else cared for (or cares for, if ongoing) your child? When? How did (or do) you feel about this? | |
| Intergenerational issues, culture, and values | Are you raising _____ in the same way that you were raised or in a different way? Do you follow your parents' customs? What languages do you speak at home? | |
| Caregiving needs | What are _____'s special needs? | |

**13–18 MONTHS**

# Reflective Parent Interview for Subsequent Visits

## Supervisor to the direct care practitioner:

*What seemed most important in the parent's responses to the questions? We will write these replies in the child's record. Did the parent interact with the child during the interview? If so, we will need to describe these interactions in the child's chart as well.*

| Interview area | Question(s) | Notes and observations |
| --- | --- | --- |
| Family relationships | How are things going at home? | |
| Role as a parent | How do you feel now that you have been a parent for a while? | |
| Child's ongoing health and development | Do you have any new concerns about _____'s health or development? | |
| Family supports | Is your family supporting you? If so, how? | |
| Parent's understanding of the child's cues | Have you noticed any changes in the way that _____ lets you know what he or she wants or needs? Have you made any changes in the way that you are responding to _____? | |
| Relationship with the child care program | How has _____ been responding to the way that we are working with him or her? Have you felt included? | |
| Intergenerational issues, culture, and values | What kinds of things are you and _____ doing together at home? Are you raising _____ in the same way that you were raised or in a different way? | |
| Caregiving needs | Does _____ have any special needs at this time? | |

# SYNTHESIS

*We will now synthesize our observations from the meeting with the information gained during the reflective parent interview to address four areas in the spaces that follow. The answers to these questions, illustrated by our concrete observations, structure the letter for the parent.*

1. How did the child demonstrate strengths in his or her responses to the tasks, to the parent, and to us? How did the child coordinate his or her systems, and did the child initiate without prompting from the parent or supervisor?

2. How were these behaviors related to the interactions that we observed between the parent and child? How did the child contribute to these interactions?

3. Does the parent have any special concerns? How did we agree with the parent to respond to these concerns?

4. Are we concerned about the child's development in any way? If so, how can we suggest working with the family to strengthen the child's development within his or her social-cultural community?

*The Visit: Observation, Reflection, Synthesis for Training and Relationship Building*, by Annette Axtmann and Annegret Dettwiler.

**SUPERVISOR TO THE DIRECT CARE PRACTITIONER:**

*How do you feel about working with this family?*

*I will transform our notes into the letter for the parent. Once you read and approve the letter, I'll ask you to sign it as well. Please let me know what you continue to observe on a daily basis. We will meet again to reflect together on this family and what we have learned about the family today, as well as what you are observing on a daily basis.*

## FUTURE SUPERVISION FOR DIRECT CARE PRACTITIONER FORM

NAME OF PRACTITIONER: _____

DATE OF VISIT: _____

NUMBER OF VISIT FOR PRACTITIONER: _____

CHILD'S AND PARENT'S NAMES: _____

_____

_____

The following sections detail the direct care practitioner's areas of strength and areas for future observation and follow-up.

**DURING THE MEETING**

Observe the child and parent before interacting with them; this will allow your behavior to be tuned to the child and parent.

| Areas of strength | Areas for future observation and follow-up |
|---|---|
|  |  |

Reflect before answering questions posed by the supervisor and illustrate answers (in part) with nonevaluative observations.

| Areas of strength | Areas for future observation and follow-up |
|---|---|
| | |

Describe systems used and/or systems not used by the child during tasks and during self-initiated behavior.

| Areas of strength | Areas for future observation and follow-up |
|---|---|
| | |

Relate observations to the child's history as told by the parent during the reflective parent interview (or related by the supervisor) that contribute to the synthesis of information collected from child and parent during the meeting.

| Areas of strength | Areas for future observation and follow-up |
|---|---|
| | |

Suggest one or two ways—based on observations and synthesis—to work with the family.

| Areas of strength | Areas for future observation and follow-up |
|---|---|
| | |

Relate knowledge of the nonlinear dynamic systems perspective of child development and basic principles of development to aspects of the child's and/or parent's behavior.

| Areas of strength | Areas for future observation and follow-up |
|---|---|
| | |

Child's name: _____

Child's date of birth: _____

Date of visit: _____

## Age Range: 18–24 months

## FOR THE SUPERVISOR

The Visit is an opportunity for you to provide in-service training for caregivers, home visitors, social services coordinators, and family child care providers and for you to strengthen your work with families. These goals will be accomplished through

OBSERVATION    REFLECTION    SYNTHESIS

## PREPARE FOR THE MEETING:

- Review the child's medical record, enrollment form, and/or prior records from the Visit.
- Obtain a blank copy of the appropriate-age Guide by photocopying it from the book or printing it from the accompanying CD-ROM.
- Fill in the child's name throughout the Guide.
- Secure the materials needed for the tasks. These vary according to the child's age range; see the Meeting section of this Guide for the task-specific materials.
- Prioritize the interview questions according to which issues might be most important for the family.
- Consider how the direct care practitioner will be included throughout the meeting with the family.

## DURING THE MEETING:

- Observe interactions among the direct care practitioner, the child, the parent, and, if present, other family members. Be guided by your observations.
- Ask the parent to choose whether to begin with the reflective parent interview or tasks for the child.
- Observe parent–child interactions. Comment *in the moment* on beneficial interactions. Doing so will empower the parent and instruct the direct care practitioner.
- Observe which systems (social-emotional, visual, motor, cognitive, communication) the child uses to solve the task, and how the child solves the task.
- Observe which system(s) the child does not use to solve the task.
- Observe the child's self-initiated behavior and ask yourself how the child's behavior relates to parent–child interactions.
- Pause after each interview question to give the parent time to reflect.
- Do not take notes during the meeting. (Notes can be taken during the co-review.)

## DURING THE CO-REVIEW:

- Ask the direct care practitioner questions as listed in the co-review section of this Guide, and use his or her answers to guide the co-review.
- Share concrete observations, and reflect together on how they relate to
  - The parent–child relationship
  - The child's use of social-emotional, visual, motor, cognitive, and communication systems during tasks
  - The child's self-initiated behavior

---

**18–24 MONTHS**

2

- Use the Visit's Developmental Characteristics Chart to compare the child's behavior to that of others in his or her age range.

### SYNTHESIZE:

- Synthesize the parent's responses during the reflective parent interview with observations made by the team during the meeting. Observations should include which systems the child used or did not use and the child's behavior as compared with others in his or her age range.
- Use the synthesis to write a letter for the parent. The letter should summarize what you and the direct care practitioner have learned and how you have agreed with the parent to work for the child's benefit. Illustrate the letter with observations made by you and the direct care practitioner.
- Fill out the Future Supervision for Direct Care Practitioner Form.

*Remember that how you act is as important as what you do.*

# Meeting
## Age Range: 18–24 Months

**Materials:**

Ball, cubes, two cups, crayon, paper, doll, bowl, spoon

**Create a space (in the home or child care setting) to administer the Visit:**

Identify a space in which the child can move freely. Identify stairs for the child to climb, if possible. Clear a space on an adult-size table.

**Supervisor to the direct care practitioner:**

*You are here to exchange information with the family because you provide direct care for the child—meaning that the family considers you a very important person in the service system. There are two parts to our meeting with the family: 1) tasks for the child and 2) a reflective parent interview. During the interview, allow the child to explore and to interact with his or her parent naturally. Please allow the child to cry, crawl, or walk to establish contact with his or her parent. Do not pull the child back or ask the parent for help. We want to observe how the parent responds—or does not respond—to the child while he or she is answering sensitive questions. We need to observe how the parent and child interact because the child's growth and development depend on parent–child interactions.*

**Supervisor to the parent:**

*Welcome. You were asked to participate in this meeting so that we can exchange information and share the care of your child with you. We will administer some developmental tasks to determine _____'s individual competencies. As you are part of _____'s family, we will ask you some questions about him or her. Please care for _____ or ask the direct care practitioner to do so when you feel it is best. We will observe how you interact with _____ so that we can perhaps imitate you while we are caring for him or her. This meeting takes approximately 30 minutes. Would you prefer to begin with the interview questions or the tasks?*

**Overall directions for the supervisor during the meeting:**

- Remember that observations are nonevaluative; they will be interpreted and discussed during the co-review.
- Ask all participants to sit on the floor, at the child's eye level.
- Observe the child's eye contact, smiles, and vocalizations.
- Compare the child's reactions to the parent (as a familiar person) and to you (as a stranger).
- Observe and comment on the competence expressed by the child's self-initiated behaviors.

---

*The Visit: Observation, Reflection, Synthesis for Training and Relationship Building,* by Annette Axtmann and Annegret Dettwiler.

- Ask the parent to administer the tasks that are italicized in the chart, and do not interfere when the parent administers a task.
- If the child does not do a task, ask the parent if the child does it at home.

## WHAT TO LOOK FOR DURING PARENT–CHILD INTERACTIONS:
- Clarity of the child's behavior toward the parent (e.g., eye contact, vocalizations, body movement)
- Contingent parent responses to the child
- Noncontingent parent responses to the child
- No parent response to the child (i.e., parent ignores the child)
- Child self-initiated actions (i.e., whether the parent permits them)
- Cultural aspects of parent–child interactions

## TASKS
### GUIDELINES FOR ADMINISTERING AND OBSERVING PERFORMANCE OF THE TASKS

| Task and related systems | Cues for administration | Strengths and needs to observe as the child responds to the tasks |
|---|---|---|
| **Walks and runs**<br>Motor<br>Cognitive<br>Visual | Ask the child to walk and run.<br>Observe how the child coordinates his or her individual body segments as he or she walks or runs around tables and chairs. | Coordination of motor and visual systems |
| **Walks up and down stairs**<br>Motor<br>Cognitive<br>Visual | Ask the child to walk up and down the stairs.<br>Observe whether the child holds on to the railing or an adult's hand.<br>Observe whether the child alternates his or her feet. | Coordination of motor, cognitive, and visual systems |
| **Kicks**<br>Motor<br>Visual<br>Cognitive | *Ask the parent to place a ball in front of the child's feet.*<br>*Ask the parent to ask the child to kick the ball.*<br>Observe the child's steadiness while kicking. | Coordination of visual and motor systems |

*The Visit: Observation, Reflection, Synthesis for Training and Relationship Building*, by Annette Axtmann and Annegret Dettwiler.

**18–24 MONTHS**

| Task and related systems | Cues for administration | Strengths and needs to observe as the child responds to the tasks |
|---|---|---|
| **Manipulates cubes**<br>Cognitive<br>Motor<br>Visual | *Ask the parent to help the child onto his or her lap or into a high chair at the table.*<br>Offer the child six cubes, one at a time.<br>Observe the child's grasp as he or she manipulates the cubes.<br>Observe whether the child stacks the cubes on his or her own initiative.<br>Demonstrate if the child does not stack the cubes on his or her own initiative.<br>Observe whether the child imitates. | Relationship between inanimate objects<br>Coordination of motor and visual systems<br>Imitation |
| **Find a cube under one of two cups**<br>Cognitive<br>Motor<br>Visual | Hide a cube under one of the two cups while the child is watching.<br>Ask the child to find the cube.<br>Hide the cube again, and reverse the position of the cups by sliding them past each other on the table.<br>Ask the child to find the cube.<br>Repeat this activity at least one more time to avoid accidental solutions on the child's part. | Object permanence<br>Coordination of motor and visual systems |
| **Imitates drawing a line**<br>Cognitive<br>Motor<br>Visual | Draw a single vertical line on a piece of paper.<br>Offer the crayon to the child.<br>Observe whether the child imitates drawing a vertical line.<br>Repeat the activity, this time by drawing a single horizontal line.<br>Observe the child's grasp of the crayon.<br>Observe whether the child imitates drawing a horizontal line. | Coordination of visual and motor systems<br>Adaptation of grasp |
| **Identifies familiar objects and/or body parts**<br>Communication<br>Cognitive<br>Visual | *Ask the parent to encourage the child to point to or name familiar objects in the environment.*<br>*Ask the parent to encourage the child to point to or name body parts on him- or herself or the doll.* | Coordination of visual, cognitive, and communication systems |

*The Visit: Observation, Reflection, Synthesis for Training and Relationship Building,* by Annette Axtmann and Annegret Dettwiler.

| Task and related systems | Cues for administration | Strengths and needs to observe as the child responds to the tasks |
| --- | --- | --- |
| **Follows directions and engages in pretend play**<br>Social-emotional<br>Cognitive<br>Communication<br>Motor<br>Visual | *Ask the parent to encourage the child to feed the doll with the spoon (without a demonstration).*<br>Observe the child's grasp of the spoon.<br>Observe whether the child engages in pretend play.<br>Observe for the child's spontaneous production of words. | Coordination of social-emotional, communication, and motor systems<br>Manipulation of spoon (adaptive) |
| **Demonstrates self-help skills**<br>Motor | Observe whether the child participates in dressing him- or herself. | Coordination of motor and cognitive systems (adaptive skills) |

*The Visit: Observation, Reflection, Synthesis for Training and Relationship Building,* by Annette Axtmann and Annegret Dettwiler.
© 2005 Paul H. Brookes Publishing Co. All rights reserved.

**18–24** MONTHS

# REFLECTIVE PARENT INTERVIEW

## QUESTIONS FOR THE FIRST VISIT

Please use the following script as a guide only. Prioritize the order of the questions according to what you already know and are learning about the child and parent during this meeting with them. Wait for the parent to reflect and to respond fully—in whatever way seems comfortable for him or her. Remember that some questions can be left for later during the family's participation in the program. As you ask questions, observe how the parent maintains a balance between responding to the questions and to the demands made by the child. **Do not take notes.**

| INTERVIEW AREA | QUESTION(S) |
|---|---|
| Family beginnings | *How did you begin as a family?* |
| Role as a parent | *How did you feel when you found out you were going to be a parent? Did you plan to have _____?* |
| Pregnancy and delivery | *How did the pregnancy go? What was the delivery like?* |
| Family supports | *What was it like for you when you first came home with _____?* |
| Parent's understanding of the child's cues | *How does _____ tell you that he or she is hungry or tired? Please describe or mimic _____'s cries or signals regarding hunger or sleep.* |
| Separation | *Have you and _____ ever been separated? Who else has cared for (or cares for, if ongoing) your child? When? How did (or do) you feel about this?* |
| Intergenerational issues, culture, and values | *Are you raising _____ in the same way that you were raised or in a different way? Do you follow your parents' customs? What languages do you speak at home?* |
| Caregiving needs | *What are _____'s special needs?* |

## CLOSURE OF THE MEETING

*There is much more for us to learn from one another. We will write you a letter summarizing what we have learned about _____ and how we all have agreed to work with him (or her). We appreciate the time that you and _____ have spent with us. Thank you.*

# REFLECTIVE PARENT INTERVIEW

## QUESTIONS FOR SUBSEQUENT VISITS

Please use the following script as a guide only. Prioritize the order of the questions according to what you already know and are learning about the child and parent during this meeting with them. Wait for the parent to reflect and to respond fully—in whatever way seems comfortable for him or her. Remember that some questions can be left for later during the family's participation in the program. As you ask questions, observe how the parent maintains a balance between responding to the questions and to the demands made by the child. **Do not take notes.**

| INTERVIEW AREA | QUESTION(S) |
|---|---|
| Family relationships | *How are things going at home?* |
| Role as a parent | *How do you feel now that you have been a parent for a while?* |
| Child's ongoing health and development | *Do you have any new concerns about _____'s health or development?* |
| Family supports | *Is your family supporting you? If so, how?* |
| Parent's understanding of the child's cues | *Have you noticed any changes in the way that _____ lets you know what he or she wants or needs? Have you made any changes in the way that you are responding to _____?* |
| Relationship with the program | *How has _____ been responding to the way that we are working with him or her? Have you felt included?* |
| Intergenerational issues, culture, and values | *What kinds of things are you and _____ doing together at home? Are you raising _____ in the same way that you were raised or in a different way?* |
| Caregiving needs | *Does _____ have any special needs at this time?* |

## CLOSURE OF THE MEETING

*There is much more for us to learn from one another. We will write you a letter summarizing what we have learned about _____ and how we all have agreed to work with him (or her). We appreciate the time that you and _____ have spent with us. Thank you.*

## CO-REVIEW OF VISIT # _____
## FOR CHILD'S ONGOING RECORD

CHILD'S NAME: _____

DATE OF VISIT: _____

CHILD'S AGE AT TIME OF VISIT (IN MONTHS AND DAYS): _____

TEAM MEMBERS: SUPERVISOR _____

DIRECT CARE PRACTITIONER _____

NAME(S) OF CHILD'S FAMILY MEMBER(S) IN ATTENDANCE: _____

_____

_____

HEALTH ISSUES NOTED ON CHILD'S MEDICAL FORM: _____

_____

_____

**18–24 MONTHS**      10

**MATERIALS:**
Pencil, Developmental Characteristics Chart

**SUPERVISOR INTRODUCES THE CO-REVIEW TO THE DIRECT CARE PRACTITIONER:**

*During this co-review, we will share our observations of the child and his or her parent. We will relate these observations to what each of us remembers about the child's response to his or her parent and to us, the child's self-initiated behaviors, the child's performance of the tasks, and the parent's answers during the interview. In addition, we will record observations of parent–child interactions in the right-hand column of the chart that follows. Overall, we will ask the following questions during this co-review:*

- *What do the observations indicate about the child's strengths and/or needs? How were these areas of strength or need influenced by the child's interactions with his or her parent?*
- *Which systems did the child use or not use to solve the tasks?*
- *Did the child's behavior during the meeting indicate that the child's systems are in balance or off balance?*

*As we synthesize this information, we will develop a picture of the child within the context of his or her family. We will use this picture to draft a letter to the parent summarizing what we and the parent agreed to do for the child's well-being. We will illustrate the letter with our observations.*

## CHILD'S STRENGTHS AND NEEDS

**SUPERVISOR TO THE DIRECT CARE PRACTITIONER:**

*We will share our observations of how the child used his or her various systems to solve each task. This will enable us to uncover the child's strengths. If the parent reported that he or she has seen the child do the task at home, we will note that here as well.*

| Task and related systems | Observations of how the child used his or her systems | Observations of parent–child interactions during the task |
|---|---|---|
| **Walks and runs**<br>Cognitive<br>Motor<br>Visual | Did the child walk and/or run with coordination?<br>Did the child take necessary precautions to avoid running into tables, chairs, or other obstacles? | |
| **Walks up and down stairs**<br>Motor<br>Cognitive<br>Visual | Did the child walk up and down stairs while holding on to the railing or an adult's hand, or was he or she able to negotiate the stairs without support?<br>Did the child alternate his or her feet? | |
| **Kicks**<br>Motor<br>Visual<br>Cognitive | Did the child swing one leg forward to kick the ball?<br>Did the child maintain the standing position steadily while kicking?<br>Did the child attend visually to the ball? | |
| **Manipulates cubes**<br>Cognitive<br>Motor<br>Visual | How did the child grasp the cube?<br>Did the child stack a tower of six cubes on his or her own initiative?<br>Did the child imitate stacking a tower? | |
| **Finds a cube under one of two cups**<br>Cognitive<br>Motor<br>Visual | Did the child find the cube under the cup?<br>Did the child find the cube under the cup when the cups were reversed? | |
| **Imitates drawing a line**<br>Cognitive<br>Motor<br>Visual | How did the child grasp the crayon?<br>Did the child imitate drawing vertical and horizontal lines on the piece of paper? | |
| **Identifies familiar objects and/or body parts**<br>Communication<br>Cognitive<br>Visual | Did the child name familiar objects in the environment?<br>Did the child name body parts on him- or herself or the doll? | |

**18–24 MONTHS**        12

*The Visit: Observation, Reflection, Synthesis for Training and Relationship Building,* by Annette Axtmann and Annegret Dettwiler.
© 2005 Paul H. Brookes Publishing Co. All rights reserved.

| Task and related systems | Observations of how the child used his or her systems | Observations of parent–child interactions during the task |
|---|---|---|
| **Follows directions and engages in pretend play** | | |
| Social-emotional | How did the child grasp the spoon? | |
| Cognitive | Did the child engage in pretend play by feeding the doll? | |
| Communication | | |
| Motor | Did the child produce entire words during pretend play? | |
| Visual | | |
| **Demonstrates self-help skills** | | |
| Motor | Did the child participate in dressing him- or herself? | |

SUPERVISOR TO THE DIRECT CARE PRACTITIONER:

- *What are the child's strengths, and how do they seem to relate to our observations of parent–child interactions?*
- *Did the parent and child interact during the tasks, and did these interactions influence the child's performance of the tasks?*
- *Did the parent seem to understand the child's behavior?*
- *Did the parent's response mesh with the child's behavior?*
- *Did the parent ignore the child?*
- *Did the parent allow the child to self-initiate?*
- *Does it appear that the family's culture influenced interactions between the parent and child and the child's use of his or her systems?*

*Let's use the Developmental Characteristics Chart to compare the child's task performance with that of other children in the same age range. What do we learn from the comparisons?*

*The Visit: Observation, Reflection, Synthesis for Training and Relationship Building,* by Annette Axtmann and Annegret Dettwiler.

**18–24 MONTHS**

# REFLECTIVE PARENT INTERVIEW FOR THE FIRST VISIT

**SUPERVISOR TO THE DIRECT CARE PRACTITIONER:**

*What seemed most important in the parent's responses to the questions? We will write these replies in the child's record. Did the parent interact with the child during the interview? If so, we will need to describe these interactions in the child's record as well.*

| Interview area | Question(s) | Notes and observations |
|---|---|---|
| Family beginnings | How did you begin as a family? | |
| Role as a parent | How did you feel when you found out you were going to be a parent? Did you plan to have _____? | |
| Pregnancy and delivery | How did the pregnancy go? What was the delivery like? | |
| Family supports | What was it like for you when you first came home with _____? | |
| Parent's understanding of the child's cues | How does _____ tell you that he or she is hungry or tired? Please describe or mimic _____'s cries or signals regarding hunger or sleep. | |
| Separation | Have you and _____ ever been separated? Who else cared for (or cares for, if ongoing) your child? When? How did (or do) you feel about this? | |
| Intergenerational issues, culture, and values | Are you raising _____ in the same way that you were raised or in a different way? Do you follow your parents' customs? What languages do you speak at home? | |
| Caregiving needs | What are _____'s special needs? | |

# REFLECTIVE PARENT INTERVIEW FOR SUBSEQUENT VISITS

## SUPERVISOR TO THE DIRECT CARE PRACTITIONER:

*What seemed most important in the parent's responses to the questions? We will write these replies in the child's record. Did the parent interact with the child during the interview? If so, we will need to describe these interactions in the child's chart as well.*

| Interview area | Question(s) | Notes and observations |
|---|---|---|
| Family relationships | How are things going at home? | |
| Role as a parent | How do you feel now that you have been a parent for a while? | |
| Child's ongoing health and development | Do you have any new concerns about _____'s health or development? | |
| Family supports | Is your family supporting you? If so, how? | |
| Parent's understanding of the child's cues | Have you noticed any changes in the way that _____ lets you know what he or she wants or needs? Have you made any changes in the way that you are responding to _____? | |
| Relationship with the child care program | How has _____ been responding to the way that we are working with him or her? Have you felt included? | |
| Intergenerational issues, culture, and values | What kinds of things are you and _____ doing together at home? Are you raising _____ in the same way that you were raised or in a different way? | |
| Caregiving needs | Does _____ have any special needs at this time? | |

18–24 MONTHS

*The Visit: Observation, Reflection, Synthesis for Training and Relationship Building,* by Annette Axtmann and Annegret Dettwiler.

# Synthesis

**Supervisor to the direct care practitioner:**

*We will now synthesize our observations from the meeting with the information gained during the reflective parent interview to address four areas in the spaces that follow. The answers to these questions, illustrated by our concrete observations, structure the letter for the parent.*

1.   How did the child demonstrate strengths in his or her responses to the tasks, to the parent, and to us? How did the child coordinate his or her systems, and did the child initiate without prompting from the parent or supervisor?

2.   How were these behaviors related to the interactions that we observed between the parent and child? How did the child contribute to these interactions?

    *The Visit: Observation, Reflection, Synthesis for Training and Relationship Building*, by Annette Axtmann and Annegret Dettwiler.

3. Does the parent have any special concerns? How did we agree with the parent to respond to these concerns?

4. Are we concerned about the child's development in any way? If so, how can we suggest working with the family to strengthen the child's development within his or her social-cultural community?

# CLOSURE

**SUPERVISOR TO THE DIRECT CARE PRACTITIONER:**
*How do you feel about working with this family?*

*I will transform our notes into the letter for the parent. Once you read and approve the letter, I'll ask you to sign it as well. Please let me know what you continue to observe on a daily basis. We will meet again to reflect together on this family and what we have learned about the family today, as well as what you are observing on a daily basis.*

---

**18–24 MONTHS**                    18

# Future Supervision for Direct Care Practitioner Form

NAME OF PRACTITIONER: _____

DATE OF VISIT: _____

NUMBER OF VISIT FOR PRACTITIONER: _____

CHILD'S AND PARENT'S NAMES: _____

_____

_____

The following sections detail the direct care practitioner's areas of strength and areas for future observation and follow-up.

## DURING THE MEETING

Observe the child and parent before interacting with them; this will allow your behavior to be tuned to the child and parent.

| Areas of strength | Areas for future observation and follow-up |
|---|---|
|  |  |

**18–24 MONTHS**

Reflect before answering questions posed by the supervisor and illustrate answers (in part) with nonevaluative observations.

| Areas of strength | Areas for future observation and follow-up |
| --- | --- |
|  |  |

Describe systems used and/or systems not used by the child during tasks and during self-initiated behavior.

| Areas of strength | Areas for future observation and follow-up |
| --- | --- |
|  |  |

Relate observations to the child's history as told by the parent during the reflective parent interview (or related by the supervisor) that contribute to the synthesis of information collected from child and parent during the meeting.

| Areas of strength | Areas for future observation and follow-up |
| --- | --- |
|  |  |

Suggest one or two ways—based on observations and synthesis—to work with the family.

| Areas of strength | Areas for future observation and follow-up |
|---|---|
| | |

Relate knowledge of the nonlinear dynamic systems perspective of child development and basic principles of development to aspects of the child's and/or parent's behavior.

| Areas of strength | Areas for future observation and follow-up |
|---|---|
| | |

*The Visit: Observation, Reflection, Synthesis for Training and Relationship Building,* by Annette Axtmann and Annegret Dettwiler.
© 2005 Paul H. Brookes Publishing Co. All rights reserved.

**18–24 MONTHS**

## OBSERVATION, REFLECTION, SYNTHESIS GUIDE AND VISIT RECORD FOR

CHILD'S NAME: _____

CHILD'S DATE OF BIRTH: _____

DATE OF VISIT: _____

### AGE RANGE: 24–30 MONTHS

## For the supervisor

The Visit is an opportunity for you to provide in-service training for caregivers, home visitors, social services coordinators, and family child care providers and for you to strengthen your work with families. These goals will be accomplished through

OBSERVATION  REFLECTION  SYNTHESIS

### Prepare for the meeting:

- Review the child's medical record, enrollment form, and/or prior records from the Visit.
- Obtain a blank copy of the appropriate-age Guide by photocopying it from the book or printing it from the accompanying CD-ROM.
- Fill in the child's name throughout the Guide.
- Secure the materials needed for the tasks. These vary according to the child's age range; see the Meeting section of this Guide for the task-specific materials.
- Prioritize the interview questions according to which issues might be most important for the family.
- Consider how the direct care practitioner will be included throughout the meeting with the family.

### During the meeting:

- Observe interactions among the direct care practitioner, the child, the parent, and, if present, other family members. Be guided by your observations.
- Ask the parent to choose whether to begin with the reflective parent interview or tasks for the child.
- Observe parent–child interactions. Comment *in the moment* on beneficial interactions. Doing so will empower the parent and instruct the direct care practitioner.
- Observe which systems (social-emotional, visual, motor, cognitive, communication) the child uses to solve the task, and how the child solves the task.
- Observe which system(s) the child does not use to solve the task.
- Observe the child's self-initiated behavior and ask yourself how the child's behavior relates to parent–child interactions.
- Pause after each interview question to give the parent time to reflect.
- Do not take notes during the meeting. (Notes can be taken during the co-review.)

### During the co-review:

- Ask the direct care practitioner questions as listed in the co-review section of this Guide, and use his or her answers to guide the co-review.
- Share concrete observations, and reflect together on how they relate to
  - The parent–child relationship
  - The child's use of social-emotional, visual, motor, cognitive, and communication systems during tasks
  - The child's self-initiated behavior

---

**24–30 MONTHS**

2

- Use the Visit's Developmental Characteristics Chart to compare the child's behavior to that of others in his or her age range.

### SYNTHESIZE:

- Synthesize the parent's responses during the reflective parent interview with observations made by the team during the meeting. Observations should include which systems the child used or did not use and the child's behavior as compared with others in his or her age range.
- Use the synthesis to write a letter for the parent. The letter should summarize what you and the direct care practitioner have learned and how you have agreed with the parent to work for the child's benefit. Illustrate the letter with observations made by you and the direct care practitioner.
- Fill out the Future Supervision for Direct Care Practitioner Form.

*Remember that how you act is as important as what you do.*

# MEETING

## AGE RANGE: 24–30 MONTHS

**MATERIALS:**

Ball, cubes, crayon, paper, picture book, Cheerios, bowl, spoon

**CREATE A SPACE (IN THE HOME OR
CHILD CARE SETTING) TO ADMINISTER THE VISIT:**

Identify a space in which the child can move freely. Identify stairs for the child to climb, if possible. Clear a space on an adult-size table.

**SUPERVISOR TO THE DIRECT CARE PRACTITIONER:**

*You are here to exchange information with the family because you provide direct care for the child—meaning that the family considers you a very important person in the service system. There are two parts to our meeting with the family: 1) tasks for the child and 2) a reflective parent interview. During the interview, allow the child to explore and to interact with his or her parent naturally. Please allow the child to cry, crawl, or walk to establish contact with his or her parent. Do not pull the child back or ask the parent for help. We want to observe how the parent responds—or does not respond—to the child while he or she is answering sensitive questions. We need to observe how the parent and child interact because the child's growth and development depend on parent–child interactions.*

**SUPERVISOR TO THE PARENT:**

*Welcome. You were asked to participate in this meeting so that we can exchange information and share the care of your child with you. We will administer some developmental tasks to determine _____'s individual competencies. As you are part of _____'s family, we will ask you some questions about him or her. Please care for _____ or ask the direct care practitioner to do so when you feel it is best. We will observe how you interact with _____ so that we can perhaps imitate you while we are caring for him or her. This meeting takes approximately 30 minutes. Would you prefer to begin with the interview questions or the tasks?*

**OVERALL DIRECTIONS FOR THE SUPERVISOR DURING THE MEETING:**

- Remember that observations are nonevaluative; they will be interpreted and discussed during the co-review.
- Ask all participants to sit on the floor, at the child's eye level.
- Observe the child's eye contact, smiles, and vocalizations.
- Compare the child's reactions to the parent (as a familiar person) and to you (as a stranger).
- Observe and comment on the competence expressed by the child's self-initiated behaviors.

- Ask the parent to administer the tasks that are italicized in the chart, and do not interfere when the parent administers a task.
- If the child does not do a task, ask the parent if the child does it at home.

**WHAT TO LOOK FOR DURING PARENT–CHILD INTERACTIONS:**
- Clarity of the child's behavior toward the parent (e.g., eye contact, vocalizations, body movement)
- Contingent parent responses to the child
- Noncontingent parent responses to the child
- No parent response to the child (i.e., parent ignores the child)
- Child self-initiated actions (i.e., whether the parent permits them)
- Cultural aspects of parent–child interactions

## TASKS
### GUIDELINES FOR ADMINISTERING AND OBSERVING PERFORMANCE OF THE TASKS

| Task and related systems | Cues for administration | Strengths and needs to observe as the child responds to the tasks |
|---|---|---|
| **Walks up and down stairs**<br>Motor<br>Cognitive<br>Visual | Ask the child to walk up and down the stairs.<br>Observe whether the child holds on to the railing or an adult's hand.<br>Observe whether the child alternates his or her feet. | Coordination of motor, cognitive, and visual systems |
| **Jumps**<br>Motor<br>Cognitive<br>Visual | Ask the child to jump from a low step or stool to the floor.<br>Ask the child to jump up and down on the floor.<br>Offer assistance if necessary. | Coordination of motor, cognitive, and visual systems |
| **Kicks**<br>Motor<br>Cognitive<br>Visual | *Ask the parent to place the ball in front of the child's feet.*<br>*Ask the parent to encourage the child to kick the ball.*<br>Observe the child's steadiness while kicking. | Coordination of motor, cognitive, and visual systems |

| Task and related systems | Cues for administration | Strengths and needs to observe as the child responds to the tasks |
|---|---|---|
| **Builds structures with cubes**<br>Cognitive<br>Motor<br>Visual | *Ask the parent to help the child onto his or her lap or into a high chair at the table.*<br>Use the cubes to construct a train on the table, then say, "Choo-choo!"<br>Offer the cubes to the child and say, "You can make a train, too."<br>Observe the child's response. | Coordination of motor and visual systems<br>Imaginary play<br>Relationship between inanimate objects |
| **Imitates drawing a circle**<br>Cognitive<br>Motor<br>Visual | Draw a circle on a piece of paper.<br>Offer the crayon to the child.<br>Observe whether the child imitates.<br>Observe the child's grasp of the crayon. | Coordination of visual and motor systems<br>Adaptation of grasp (adaptive)<br>Imitation |
| **Asks questions and combines words**<br>Communication<br>Cognitive<br>Visual<br>Social-emotional | Observe whether the child asks questions or combines two or more words on his or her own initiative.<br>Offer the parent the picture book.<br>*Ask the parent to talk with the child about the book.*<br>Observe the child's participation. | Coordination of visual, cognitive, communication, and social-emotional systems |
| **Demonstrates self-help skills and engages in pretend play**<br>Social-emotional<br>Motor<br>Cognitive<br>Visual | *Ask the parent to offer the child pretend food on a spoon.*<br>Observe how the child pretends to eat, either independently or with assistance.<br>Note the child's grasp of the spoon.<br>*Ask the parent to describe the child's pretend play at home.*<br>*Ask the parent whether the child helps around the house (e.g., carries a dirty plate to the kitchen sink).* | Coordination of social-emotional, visual, communication, motor, and cognitive systems<br>Cognitive systems (adaptive) |

*The Visit: Observation, Reflection, Synthesis for Training and Relationship Building,* by Annette Axtmann and Annegret Dettwiler.

# Reflective Parent Interview

## Questions for the first Visit

Please use the following script as a guide only. Prioritize the order of the questions according to what you already know and are learning about the child and parent during this meeting with them. Wait for the parent to reflect and to respond fully—in whatever way seems comfortable for him or her. Remember that some questions can be left for later during the family's participation in the program. As you ask questions, observe how the parent maintains a balance between responding to the questions and to the demands made by the child. **Do not take notes.**

| Interview area | Question(s) |
|---|---|
| Family beginnings | *How did you begin as a family?* |
| Role as a parent | *How did you feel when you found out you were going to be a parent? Did you plan to have _____?* |
| Pregnancy and delivery | *How did the pregnancy go? What was the delivery like?* |
| Family supports | *What was it like for you when you first came home with _____?* |
| Parent's understanding of the child's cues | *How does _____ tell you that he or she is hungry or tired? Please describe or mimic _____'s cries or signals regarding hunger or sleep.* |
| Separation | *Have you and _____ ever been separated? Who else has cared for (or cares for, if ongoing) your child? When? How did (or do) you feel about this?* |
| Intergenerational issues, culture, and values | *Are you raising _____ in the same way that you were raised or in a different way? Do you follow your parents' customs? What languages do you speak at home?* |
| Caregiving needs | *What are _____'s special needs?* |

## Closure of the meeting

*There is much more for us to learn from one another. We will write you a letter summarizing what we have learned about _____ and how we all have agreed to work with him (or her). We appreciate the time that you and _____ have spent with us. Thank you.*

# REFLECTIVE PARENT INTERVIEW

## QUESTIONS FOR SUBSEQUENT VISITS

Please use the following script as a guide only. Prioritize the order of the questions according to what you already know and are learning about the child and parent during this meeting with them. Wait for the parent to reflect and to respond fully—in whatever way seems comfortable for him or her. Remember that some questions can be left for later during the family's participation in the program. As you ask questions, observe how the parent maintains a balance between responding to the questions and to the demands made by the child. **Do not take notes.**

| INTERVIEW AREA | QUESTION(S) |
|---|---|
| Family relationships | *How are things going at home?* |
| Role as a parent | *How do you feel now that you have been a parent for a while?* |
| Child's ongoing health and development | *Do you have any new concerns about _____'s health or development?* |
| Family supports | *Is your family supporting you? If so, how?* |
| Parent's understanding of the child's cues | *Have you noticed any changes in the way that _____ lets you know what he or she wants or needs? Have you made any changes in the way that you are responding to _____?* |
| Relationship with the program | *How has _____ been responding to the way that we are working with him or her? Have you felt included?* |
| Intergenerational issues, culture, and values | *What kinds of things are you and _____ doing together at home? Are you raising _____ in the same way that you were raised or in a different way?* |
| Caregiving needs | *Does _____ have any special needs at this time?* |

## CLOSURE OF THE MEETING

*There is much more for us to learn from one another. We will write you a letter summarizing what we have learned about _____ and how we all have agreed to work with him (or her). We appreciate the time that you and _____ have spent with us. Thank you.*

*The Visit: Observation, Reflection, Synthesis for Training and Relationship Building,* by Annette Axtmann and Annegret Dettwiler.

## CO-REVIEW OF VISIT # _____
## FOR CHILD'S ONGOING RECORD

CHILD'S NAME: _____

DATE OF VISIT: _____

CHILD'S AGE AT TIME OF VISIT (IN MONTHS AND DAYS): _____

TEAM MEMBERS: SUPERVISOR _____

DIRECT CARE PRACTITIONER _____

NAME(S) OF CHILD'S FAMILY MEMBER(S) IN ATTENDANCE: _____
_____
_____

HEALTH ISSUES NOTED ON CHILD'S MEDICAL FORM: _____
_____
_____

**MATERIALS:**

Pencil, Developmental Characteristics Chart

**SUPERVISOR INTRODUCES THE CO-REVIEW TO THE DIRECT CARE PRACTITIONER:**

*During this co-review, we will share our observations of the child and his or her parent. We will relate these observations to what each of us remembers about the child's response to his or her parent and to us, the child's self-initiated behaviors, the child's performance of the tasks, and the parent's answers during the interview. In addition, we will record observations of parent–child interactions in the right-hand column of the chart that follows. Overall, we will ask the following questions during this co-review:*

- *What do the observations indicate about the child's strengths and/or needs? How were these areas of strength or need influenced by the child's interactions with his or her parent?*
- *Which systems did the child use or not use to solve the tasks?*
- *Did the child's behavior during the meeting indicate that the child's systems are in balance or off balance?*

*As we synthesize this information, we will develop a picture of the child within the context of his or her family. We will use this picture to draft a letter to the parent summarizing what we and the parent agreed to do for the child's well-being. We will illustrate the letter with our observations.*

## CHILD'S STRENGTHS AND NEEDS

**SUPERVISOR TO THE DIRECT CARE PRACTITIONER:**

*We will share our observations of how the child used his or her various systems to solve each task. This will enable us to uncover the child's strengths. If the parent reported that he or she has seen the child do the task at home, we will note that here as well.*

---

**24–30 MONTHS**

10

*The Visit: Observation, Reflection, Synthesis for Training and Relationship Building*, by Annette Axtmann and Annegret Dettwiler.

| Task and related systems | Observations of how the child used his or her systems | Observations of parent–child interactions during the task |
|---|---|---|
| **Walks up and down stairs**<br>Motor<br>Cognitive<br>Visual | How did the child coordinate his or her systems while walking up and down the stairs?<br>Did the child hold on to the railing or an adult's hand, or was he or she able to negotiate the stairs without support?<br>Did the child alternate feet? | |
| **Jumps**<br>Motor<br>Cognitive<br>Visual | How did the child coordinate his or her systems while jumping from the stool or step?<br>Did the child jump on the floor with both feet off the floor at the same time?<br>Did the child need assistance? | |
| **Kicks**<br>Motor<br>Cognitive<br>Visual | Did the child swing one leg forward to kick the ball?<br>Did the child maintain the standing position steadily while kicking?<br>Did the child attend visually to the ball? | |
| **Builds structures with cubes**<br>Cognitive<br>Motor<br>Visual | Did the child imitate building a train?<br>Did the child make a train sound?<br>How did the child coordinate his or her systems during this task? | |
| **Imitates drawing a circle**<br>Cognitive<br>Motor<br>Visual | How did the child coordinate his or her systems while grasping the crayon?<br>Did the child imitate drawing a circle on a piece of paper? | |

| Task and related systems | Observations of how the child used his or her systems | Observations of parent–child interactions during the task |
|---|---|---|
| **Asks questions and combines words**<br>Communication<br>Cognitive<br>Visual<br>Social-emotional | Did the child combine two or more words on his or her own initiative?<br>Did the child participate in a conversation with his or her parent about the book?<br>Did the child ask a question on his or her own initiative?<br>Did the child respond to questions asked by the supervisor or the parent? | |
| **Demonstrates self-help skills and engages in pretend play**<br>Social-emotional<br>Motor<br>Cognitive<br>Visual | How did the child coordinate his or her systems to grasp the spoon?<br>Did the child "eat" independently?<br>How did child "eat"?<br>Does the child help his or her parent around the house?<br>Does the child engage in pretend play and use a sequence of words while doing so? | |

SUPERVISOR TO THE DIRECT CARE PRACTITIONER:

- *What are the child's strengths, and how do they seem to relate to our observations of parent–child interactions?*
- *Did the parent and child interact during the tasks, and did these interactions influence the child's performance of the tasks?*
- *Did the parent seem to understand the child's behavior?*
- *Did the parent's response mesh with the child's behavior?*
- *Did the parent ignore the child?*
- *Did the parent allow the child to self-initiate?*
- *Does it appear that the family's culture influenced interactions between the parent and child and the child's use of his or her systems?*

*Let's use the Developmental Characteristics Chart to compare the child's task performance with that of other children in the same age range. What do we learn from the comparisons?*

*The Visit: Observation, Reflection, Synthesis for Training and Relationship Building,* by Annette Axtmann and Annegret Dettwiler.

# REFLECTIVE PARENT INTERVIEW FOR THE FIRST VISIT

**SUPERVISOR TO THE DIRECT CARE PRACTITIONER:**

*What seemed most important in the parent's responses to the questions? We will write these replies in the child's record. Did the parent interact with the child during the interview? If so, we will need to describe these interactions in the child's record as well.*

| Interview area | Question(s) | Notes and observations |
|---|---|---|
| Family beginnings | How did you begin as a family? | |
| Role as a parent | How did you feel when you found out you were going to be a parent? Did you plan to have _____? | |
| Pregnancy and delivery | How did the pregnancy go? What was the delivery like? | |
| Family supports | What was it like for you when you first came home with _____? | |
| Parent's understanding of the child's cues | How does _____ tell you that he or she is hungry or tired? Please describe or mimic _____'s cries or signals regarding hunger or sleep. | |
| Separation | Have you and _____ ever been separated? Who else cared for (or cares for, if ongoing) your child? When? How did (or do) you feel about this? | |
| Intergenerational issues, culture, and values | Are you raising _____ in the same way that you were raised or in a different way? Do you follow your parents' customs? What languages do you speak at home? | |
| Caregiving needs | What are _____'s special needs? | |

*The Visit: Observation, Reflection, Synthesis for Training and Relationship Building*, by Annette Axtmann and Annegret Dettwiler.

**24–30 MONTHS**

# REFLECTIVE PARENT INTERVIEW FOR SUBSEQUENT VISITS

**SUPERVISOR TO THE DIRECT CARE PRACTITIONER:**

*What seemed most important in the parent's responses to the questions? We will write these replies in the child's record. Did the parent interact with the child during the interview? If so, we will need to describe these interactions in the child's chart as well.*

| Interview area | Question(s) | Notes and observations |
|---|---|---|
| Family relationships | How are things going at home? | |
| Role as a parent | How do you feel now that you have been a parent for a while? | |
| Child's ongoing health and development | Do you have any new concerns about _____'s health or development? | |
| Family supports | Is your family supporting you? If so, how? | |
| Parent's understanding of the child's cues | Have you noticed any changes in the way that _____ lets you know what he or she wants or needs? Have you made any changes in the way that you are responding to _____? | |
| Relationship with the child care program | How has _____ been responding to the way that we are working with him or her? Have you felt included? | |
| Intergenerational issues, culture, and values | What kinds of things are you and _____ doing together at home? Do you find that you are raising _____ in the same way that you were raised or in a different way? | |
| Caregiving needs | Does _____ have any special needs at this time? | |

*The Visit: Observation, Reflection, Synthesis for Training and Relationship Building*, by Annette Axtmann and Annegret Dettwiler.

## SYNTHESIS

*We will now synthesize our observations from the meeting with the information gained during the reflective parent interview to address four areas in the spaces that follow. The answers to these questions, illustrated by our concrete observations, structure the letter for the parent.*

1. How did the child demonstrate strengths in his or her responses to the tasks, to the parent, and to us? How did the child coordinate his or her systems, and did the child initiate without prompting from the parent or supervisor?

2. How were these behaviors related to the interactions that we observed between the parent and child? How did the child contribute to these interactions?

3. Does the parent have any special concerns? How did we agree with the parent to respond to these concerns?

4. Are we concerned about the child's development in any way? If so, how can we suggest working with the family to strengthen the child's development within his or her social-cultural community?

# CLOSURE

## SUPERVISOR TO THE DIRECT CARE PRACTITIONER:

*How do you feel about working with this family?*

*I will transform our notes into the letter for the parent. Once you read and approve the letter, I'll ask you to sign it as well. Please let me know what you continue to observe on a daily basis. We will meet again to reflect together on this family and what we have learned about the family today, as well as what you are observing on a daily basis.*

NAME OF PRACTITIONER: _____

DATE OF VISIT: _____

NUMBER OF VISIT FOR PRACTITIONER: _____

CHILD'S AND PARENT'S NAMES: _____

_____

_____

The following sections detail the direct care practitioner's areas of strength and areas for future observation and follow-up.

### DURING THE MEETING

Observe the child and parent before interacting with them; this will allow your behavior to be tuned to the child and parent.

| Areas of strength | Areas for future observation and follow-up |
|---|---|
| | |

*The Visit: Observation, Reflection, Synthesis for Training and Relationship Building,* by Annette Axtmann and Annegret Dettwiler.

Reflect before answering questions posed by the supervisor and illustrate answers (in part) with nonevaluative observations.

| Areas of strength | Areas for future observation and follow-up |
|---|---|
|  |  |

Describe systems used and/or systems not used by the child during tasks and during self-initiated behavior.

| Areas of strength | Areas for future observation and follow-up |
|---|---|
|  |  |

Relate observations to the child's history as told by the parent during the reflective parent interview (or related by the supervisor) that contribute to the synthesis of information collected from child and parent during the meeting.

| Areas of strength | Areas for future observation and follow-up |
|---|---|
|  |  |

Suggest one or two ways—based on observations and synthesis—to work with the family.

| Areas of strength | Areas for future observation and follow-up |
|---|---|
|  |  |

Relate knowledge of the nonlinear dynamic systems perspective of child development and basic principles of development to aspects of the child's and/or parent's behavior.

| Areas of strength | Areas for future observation and follow-up |
|---|---|
|  |  |

*The Visit: Observation, Reflection, Synthesis for Training and Relationship Building*, by Annette Axtmann and Annegret Dettwiler.

## OBSERVATION, REFLECTION, SYNTHESIS GUIDE AND VISIT RECORD FOR

CHILD'S NAME: _____

CHILD'S DATE OF BIRTH: _____

DATE OF VISIT: _____

## AGE RANGE: 30–36 MONTHS

## FOR THE SUPERVISOR

The Visit is an opportunity for you to provide in-service training for caregivers, home visitors, social services coordinators, and family child care providers and for you to strengthen your work with families. These goals will be accomplished through

OBSERVATION     REFLECTION     SYNTHESIS

### PREPARE FOR THE MEETING:

- Review the child's medical record, enrollment form, and/or prior records from the Visit.
- Obtain a blank copy of the appropriate-age Guide by photocopying it from the book or printing it from the accompanying CD-ROM.
- Fill in the child's name throughout the Guide.
- Secure the materials needed for the tasks. These vary according to the child's age range; see the Meeting section of this Guide for the task-specific materials.
- Prioritize the interview questions according to which issues might be most important for the family.
- Consider how the direct care practitioner will be included throughout the meeting with the family.

### DURING THE MEETING:

- Observe interactions among the direct care practitioner, the child, the parent, and, if present, other family members. Be guided by your observations.
- Ask the parent to choose whether to begin with the reflective parent interview or tasks for the child.
- Observe parent–child interactions. Comment *in the moment* on beneficial interactions. Doing so will empower the parent and instruct the direct care practitioner.
- Observe which systems (social-emotional, visual, motor, cognitive, communication) the child uses to solve the task, and how the child solves the task.
- Observe which system(s) the child does not use to solve the task.
- Observe the child's self-initiated behavior and ask yourself how the child's behavior relates to parent–child interactions.
- Pause after each interview question to give the parent time to reflect.
- Do not take notes during the meeting. (Notes can be taken during the co-review.)

### DURING THE CO-REVIEW:

- Ask the direct care practitioner questions as listed in the co-review section of this Guide, and use his or her answers to guide the co-review.
- Share concrete observations, and reflect together on how they relate to
  - The parent–child relationship
  - The child's use of social-emotional, visual, motor, cognitive, and communication systems during tasks
  - The child's self-initiated behavior

---

- Use the Visit's Developmental Characteristics Chart to compare the child's behavior to that of others in his or her age range.

### SYNTHESIZE:
- Synthesize the parent's responses during the reflective parent interview with observations made by the team during the meeting. Observations should include which systems the child used or did not use and the child's behavior as compared with others in his or her age range.
- Use the synthesis to write a letter for the parent. The letter should summarize what you and the direct care practitioner have learned and how you have agreed with the parent to work for the child's benefit. Illustrate the letter with observations made by you and the direct care practitioner.
- Fill out the Future Supervision for Direct Care Practitioner Form.

*Remember that how you act is as important as what you do.*

# MEETING
## AGE RANGE: 30–36 MONTHS

**MATERIALS:**

Ball, crayon, paper, puzzle, picture book

**CREATE A SPACE (IN THE HOME OR CHILD CARE SETTING) TO ADMINISTER THE VISIT:**

Identify a space in which the child can move freely. Identify stairs for the child to climb, if possible. Clear a space on an adult-size table.

**SUPERVISOR TO THE DIRECT CARE PRACTITIONER:**

*You are here to exchange information with the family because you provide direct care for the child—meaning that the family considers you a very important person in the service system. There are two parts to our meeting with the family: 1) tasks for the child and 2) a reflective parent interview. During the interview, allow the child to explore and to interact with his or her parent naturally. Please allow the child to cry, crawl, or walk to establish contact with his or her parent. Do not pull the child back or ask the parent for help. We want to observe how the parent responds—or does not respond—to the child while he or she is answering sensitive questions. We need to observe how the parent and child interact because the child's growth and development depend on parent–child interactions.*

**SUPERVISOR TO THE PARENT:**

*Welcome. You were asked to participate in this meeting so that we can exchange information and share the care of your child with you. We will administer some developmental tasks to determine _____'s individual competencies. As you are part of _____'s family, we will ask you some questions about him or her. Please care for _____ or ask the direct care practitioner to do so when you feel it is best. We will observe how you interact with _____ so that we can perhaps imitate you while we are caring for him or her. This meeting takes approximately 30 minutes. Would you prefer to begin with the interview questions or the tasks?*

**OVERALL DIRECTIONS FOR THE SUPERVISOR DURING THE MEETING:**

- Remember that observations are nonevaluative; they will be interpreted and discussed during the co-review.
- Ask all participants to sit on the floor, at the child's eye level.
- Observe the child's eye contact, smiles, and vocalizations.
- Compare the child's reactions to the parent (as a familiar person) and to you (as a stranger).
- Observe and comment on the competence expressed by the child's self-initiated behaviors.
- Ask the parent to administer the tasks that are italicized in the chart, and do not interfere when the parent administers a task.

---

- If the child does not do a task, ask the parent if the child does it at home.

**WHAT TO LOOK FOR DURING PARENT–CHILD INTERACTIONS:**
- Clarity of the child's behavior toward the parent (e.g., eye contact, vocalizations, body movement)
- Contingent parent responses to the child
- Noncontingent parent responses to the child
- No parent response to the child (i.e., parent ignores the child)
- Child self-initiated actions (i.e., whether the parent permits them)
- Cultural aspects of parent–child interactions

## TASKS
### GUIDELINES FOR ADMINISTERING AND OBSERVING PERFORMANCE OF THE TASKS

| Task and related systems | Cues for administration | Strengths and needs to observe as the child responds to the tasks |
| --- | --- | --- |
| **Walks up and down stairs**<br>Motor<br>Cognitive<br>Visual | Ask the child to walk up and down the stairs.<br>Observe whether the child holds on to the railing or to an adult's hand.<br>Observe whether the child alternates his or her feet. | Coordination of motor, cognitive, and visual systems |
| **Jumps**<br>Motor<br>Cognitive<br>Visual | Ask the child to jump from a low step or stool to the floor.<br>Ask the child to jump up and down on the floor.<br>Offer assistance if necessary. | Coordination of motor, cognitive, and visual systems |
| **Kicks**<br>Motor<br>Cognitive<br>Visual<br>Social-emotional | *Ask the parent to place the ball in front of the child's feet.*<br>*Ask the parent to encourage the child to kick the ball.*<br>Observe the child's steadiness while kicking. | Coordination of motor, cognitive, and visual systems |
| **Imitates drawing a circle and a cross**<br>Cognitive<br>Motor<br>Visual | Draw a circle and a cross on a piece of paper.<br>Offer the crayon to the child.<br>Observe whether the child imitates.<br>Observe the child's grasp of the crayon. | Coordination of visual and motor systems<br>Adaptation of grasp (adaptive)<br>Imitation |

| Task and related systems | Cues for administration | Strengths and needs to observe as the child responds to the tasks |
|---|---|---|
| **Problem-solves**<br>Cognitive<br>Motor<br>Visual<br>Social-emotional | *Ask the parent to offer the child a puzzle.*<br>Observe how the parent and the child solve the puzzle together. | Coordination of cognitive, visual, motor, and social-emotional systems |
| **Tells about the use of objects**<br>Communication<br>Cognitive<br>Visual | Offer the child the picture book.<br>Ask about the use of everyday objects in the book. | Coordination of visual, cognitive, and communication systems |
| **Combines words**<br>Communication<br>Cognitive | Observe whether the child combines two or more words on his or her own initiative.<br>Offer the parent the picture book.<br>*Ask the parent to talk with the child about the book.*<br>Observe the child's participation. | Coordination of visual, cognitive, and communication systems |
| **Demonstrates self-help skills and engages in pretend play**<br>Social-emotional<br>Motor<br>Visual<br>Cognitive | *Ask the parent to encourage the child to put on garments (e.g., socks) that have been removed during the completion of tasks.*<br>Observe whether the child dresses him- or herself and whether he or she needs help.<br>*Ask the parent whether the child helps around the house (e.g., carries a dirty plate to the kitchen sink).*<br>*Ask the parent to offer the child food on a spoon.*<br>*Ask the parent to describe the child's pretend play at home.* | Coordination of social-emotional, motor, visual, communication, and cognitive systems (adaptive) |

*The Visit: Observation, Reflection, Synthesis for Training and Relationship Building*, by Annette Axtmann and Annegret Dettwiler.

# REFLECTIVE PARENT INTERVIEW

## QUESTIONS FOR THE FIRST VISIT

Please use the following script as a guide only. Prioritize the order of the questions according to what you already know and are learning about the child and parent during this meeting with them. Wait for the parent to reflect and to respond fully—in whatever way seems comfortable for him or her. Remember that some questions can be left for later during the family's participation in the program. As you ask questions, observe how the parent maintains a balance between responding to the questions and to the demands made by the child. **Do not take notes.**

| INTERVIEW AREA | QUESTION(S) |
|---|---|
| Family beginnings | *How did you begin as a family?* |
| Role as a parent | *How did you feel when you found out you were going to be a parent? Did you plan to have _____?* |
| Pregnancy and delivery | *How did the pregnancy go? What was the delivery like?* |
| Family supports | *What was it like for you when you first came home with _____?* |
| Parent's understanding of the child's cues | *How does _____ tell you that he or she is hungry or tired? Please describe or mimic _____'s cries or signals regarding hunger or sleep.* |
| Separation | *Have you and _____ ever been separated? Who else has cared for (or cares for, if ongoing) your child? When? How did (or do) you feel about this?* |
| Intergenerational issues, culture, and values | *Are you raising _____ in the same way that you were raised or in a different way? Do you follow your parents' customs? What languages do you speak at home?* |
| Caregiving needs | *What are _____'s special needs?* |

## CLOSURE OF THE MEETING

*There is much more for us to learn from one another. We will write you a letter summarizing what we have learned about _____ and how we all have agreed to work with him (or her). We appreciate the time that you and _____ have spent with us. Thank you.*

# REFLECTIVE PARENT INTERVIEW

## QUESTIONS FOR SUBSEQUENT VISITS

Please use the following script as a guide only. Prioritize the order of the questions according to what you already know and are learning about the child and parent during this meeting with them. Wait for the parent to reflect and to respond fully—in whatever way seems comfortable for him or her. Remember that some questions can be left for later during the family's participation in the program. As you ask questions, observe how the parent maintains a balance between responding to the questions and to the demands made by the child. **Do not take notes.**

| INTERVIEW AREA | QUESTION(S) |
|---|---|
| Family relationships | *How are things going at home?* |
| Role as a parent | *How do you feel now that you have been a parent for a while?* |
| Child's ongoing health and development | *Do you have any new concerns about _____'s health or development?* |
| Family supports | *Is your family supporting you? If so, how?* |
| Parent's understanding of the child's cues | *Have you noticed any changes in the way that _____ lets you know what he or she wants or needs? Have you made any changes in the way that you are responding to _____?* |
| Relationship with the program | *How has _____ been responding to the way that we are working with him or her? Have you felt included?* |
| Intergenerational issues, culture, and values | *What kinds of things are you and _____ doing together at home? Are you raising _____ in the same way that you were raised or in a different way?* |
| Caregiving needs | *Does _____ have any special needs at this time?* |

## CLOSURE OF THE MEETING

*There is much more for us to learn from one another. We will write you a letter summarizing what we have learned about _____ and how we all have agreed to work with him (or her). We appreciate the time that you and _____ have spent with us. Thank you.*

*The Visit: Observation, Reflection, Synthesis for Training and Relationship Building,* by Annette Axtmann and Annegret Dettwiler.

## CO-REVIEW OF VISIT # _____
## FOR CHILD'S ONGOING RECORD

CHILD'S NAME: _____

DATE OF VISIT: _____

CHILD'S AGE AT TIME OF VISIT (IN MONTHS AND DAYS): _____

TEAM MEMBERS: SUPERVISOR _____

DIRECT CARE PRACTITIONER _____

NAME(S) OF CHILD'S FAMILY MEMBER(S) IN ATTENDANCE: _____

_____

_____

HEALTH ISSUES NOTED ON CHILD'S MEDICAL FORM: _____

_____

_____

**30–36 MONTHS**

**MATERIALS:**
Pencil, Developmental Characteristics Chart

## SUPERVISOR INTRODUCES THE CO-REVIEW TO THE DIRECT CARE PRACTITIONER:

*During this co-review, we will share our observations of the child and his or her parent. We will relate these observations to what each of us remembers about the child's response to his or her parent and to us, the child's self-initiated behaviors, the child's performance of the tasks, and the parent's answers during the interview. In addition, we will record observations of parent–child interactions in the right-hand column of the chart that follows. Overall, we will ask the following questions during this co-review:*

- *What do the observations indicate about the child's strengths and/or needs? How were these areas of strength or need influenced by the child's interactions with his or her parent?*
- *Which systems did the child use or not use to solve the tasks?*
- *Did the child's behavior during the meeting indicate that the child's systems are in balance or off balance?*

*As we synthesize this information, we will develop a picture of the child within the context of his or her family. We will use this picture to draft a letter to the parent summarizing what we and the parent agreed to do for the child's well-being. We will illustrate the letter with our observations.*

## CHILD'S STRENGTHS AND NEEDS

## SUPERVISOR TO THE DIRECT CARE PRACTITIONER:

*We will share our observations of how the child used his or her various systems to solve each task. This will enable us to uncover the child's strengths. If the parent reported that he or she has seen the child do the task at home, we will note that here as well.*

*The Visit: Observation, Reflection, Synthesis for Training and Relationship Building*, by Annette Axtmann and Annegret Dettwiler.

| Task and related systems | Observations of how the child used his or her systems | Observations of parent–child interactions during the task |
|---|---|---|
| **Walks up and down stairs**<br>Motor<br>Cognitive<br>Visual | How did the child coordinate his or her systems while walking up and down the stairs?<br>Did the child hold on to the railing or an adult, or was the child able to negotiate the stairs without support?<br>Did the child alternate his or her feet? | |
| **Jumps**<br>Motor<br>Cognitive<br>Visual | How did the child coordinate his or her systems while jumping from the stool or step?<br>Did the child jump on the floor with both feet off the floor at the same time?<br>Did the child need assistance? | |
| **Kicks**<br>Motor<br>Cognitive<br>Visual<br>Social-emotional | How did the child coordinate his or her systems while swinging one leg forward to kick the ball?<br>Did the child maintain the standing position steadily while kicking?<br>Did the child attend visually to the ball? | |
| **Imitates drawing a circle and a cross**<br>Cognitive<br>Motor<br>Visual | How did the child coordinate his or her systems while grasping the crayon?<br>Did the child imitate drawing a circle or a cross on a piece of paper? | |
| **Problem-solves**<br>Cognitive<br>Motor<br>Visual<br>Social-emotional | Did the child complete the puzzle independently?<br>Did the child and parent solve the puzzle together? | |
| **Tells about the use of objects**<br>Communication<br>Cognitive<br>Visual | How did the child describe the use of objects spontaneously?<br>Did the child respond to questions asked by the supervisor or the parent? | |

**30–36 MONTHS**

| Task and related systems | Observations of how the child used his or her systems | Observations of parent–child interactions during the task |
|---|---|---|
| **Combines words**<br>Communication<br>Cognitive | Did the child combine three to five words on his or her own initiative?<br>Did the child produce full sentences on his or her own initiative?<br>Did the child participate in a conversation with his or her parent about the book? | |
| **Demonstrates self-help skills and engages in pretend play**<br>Social-emotional<br>Motor<br>Visual<br>Cognitive | Did the child attempt to put on simple garments independently?<br>Does the child help his or her parent around house?<br>Does the child engage in pretend play and use a sequence of words while doing so? | |

SUPERVISOR TO THE DIRECT CARE PRACTITIONER:

- *What are the child's strengths, and how do they seem to relate to our observations of parent–child interactions?*
- *Did the parent and child interact during the tasks, and did these interactions influence the child's performance of the tasks?*
- *Did the parent seem to understand the child's behavior?*
- *Did the parent's response mesh with the child's behavior?*
- *Did the parent ignore the child?*
- *Did the parent allow the child to self-initiate?*
- *Does it appear that the family's culture influenced interactions between the parent and child and the child's use of his or her systems?*

*Let's use the Developmental Characteristics Chart to compare the child's task performance with that of other children in the same age range. What do we learn from the comparisons?*

*The Visit: Observation, Reflection, Synthesis for Training and Relationship Building,* by Annette Axtmann and Annegret Dettwiler.

# REFLECTIVE PARENT INTERVIEW FOR THE FIRST VISIT

**SUPERVISOR TO THE DIRECT CARE PRACTITIONER:**

*What seemed most important in the parent's responses to the questions? We will write these replies in the child's record. Did the parent interact with the child during the interview? If so, we will need to describe these interactions in the child's record as well.*

| Interview area | Question(s) | Notes and observations |
|---|---|---|
| Family beginnings | How did you begin as a family? | |
| Role as a parent | How did you feel when you found out you were going to be a parent? Did you plan to have _____? | |
| Pregnancy and delivery | How did the pregnancy go? What was the delivery like? | |
| Family supports | What was it like for you when you first came home with _____? | |
| Parent's understanding of the child's cues | How does _____ tell you that he or she is hungry or tired? Please describe or mimic _____'s cries or signals regarding hunger or sleep. | |
| Separation | Have you and _____ ever been separated? Who else cared for (or cares for, if ongoing) your child? When? How did (or do) you feel about this? | |
| Intergenerational issues, culture, and values | Are you raising _____ in the same way that you were raised or in a different way? Do you follow your parents' customs? What languages do you speak at home? | |
| Caregiving needs | What are _____'s special needs? | |

*The Visit: Observation, Reflection, Synthesis for Training and Relationship Building,* by Annette Axtmann and Annegret Dettwiler.
© 2005 Paul H. Brookes Publishing Co. All rights reserved.

**30–36 MONTHS**

# REFLECTIVE PARENT INTERVIEW FOR SUBSEQUENT VISITS

**SUPERVISOR TO THE DIRECT CARE PRACTITIONER:**

*What seemed most important in the parent's responses to the questions? We will write these replies in the child's record. Did the parent interact with the child during the interview? If so, we will need to describe these interactions in the child's chart as well.*

| Interview area | Question(s) | Notes and observations |
|---|---|---|
| Family relationships | How are things going at home? | |
| Role as a parent | How do you feel now that you have been a parent for a while? | |
| Child's ongoing health and development | Do you have any new concerns about _____'s health or development? | |
| Family supports | Is your family supporting you? If so, how? | |
| Parent's understanding of the child's cues | Have you noticed any changes in the way that _____ lets you know what he or she wants or needs? Have you made any changes in the way that you are responding to _____? | |
| Relationship with the child care program | How has _____ been responding to the way that we are working with him or her? Have you felt included? | |
| Intergenerational issues, culture, and values | What kinds of things are you and _____ doing together at home? Do you find that you are raising _____ in the same way that you were raised or in a different way? | |
| Caregiving needs | Does _____ have any special needs at this time? | |

*The Visit: Observation, Reflection, Synthesis for Training and Relationship Building,* by Annette Axtmann and Annegret Dettwiler.

# SYNTHESIS

**SUPERVISOR TO THE DIRECT CARE PRACTITIONER:**

*We will now synthesize our observations from the meeting with the information gained during the reflective parent interview to address four areas in the spaces that follow. The answers to these questions, illustrated by our concrete observations, structure the letter for the parent.*

1. How did the child demonstrate strengths in his or her responses to the tasks, to the parent, and to us? How did the child coordinate his or her systems, and did the child initiate without prompting from the parent or supervisor?

2. How were these behaviors related to the interactions that we observed between the parent and child? How did the child contribute to these interactions?

---

3. Does the parent have any special concerns? How did we agree with the parent to respond to these concerns?

4. Are we concerned about the child's development in any way? If so, how can we suggest working with the family to strengthen the child's development within his or her social-cultural community?

# CLOSURE

*How do you feel about working with this family?*

*I will transform our notes into the letter for the parent. Once you read and approve the letter, I'll ask you to sign it as well. Please let me know what you continue to observe on a daily basis. We will meet again to reflect together on this family and what we have learned about the family today, as well as what you are observing on a daily basis.*

NAME OF PRACTITIONER: _____

DATE OF VISIT: _____

NUMBER OF VISIT FOR PRACTITIONER: _____

CHILD'S AND PARENT'S NAMES: _____

_____

_____

The following sections detail the direct care practitioner's areas of strength and areas for future observation and follow-up.

## DURING THE MEETING

Observe the child and parent before interacting with them; this will allow your behavior to be tuned to the child and parent.

| Areas of strength | Areas for future observation and follow-up |
|---|---|
|  |  |

Reflect before answering questions posed by the supervisor and illustrate answers (in part) with nonevaluative observations.

| Areas of strength | Areas for future observation and follow-up |
|---|---|
|  |  |

Describe systems used and/or systems not used by the child during tasks and during self-initiated behavior.

| Areas of strength | Areas for future observation and follow-up |
|---|---|
|  |  |

Relate observations to the child's history as told by the parent during the reflective parent interview (or related by the supervisor) that contribute to the synthesis of information collected from child and parent during the meeting.

| Areas of strength | Areas for future observation and follow-up |
|---|---|
|  |  |

Suggest one or two ways—based on observations and synthesis—to work with the family.

| Areas of strength | Areas for future observation and follow-up |
| --- | --- |
| | |

Relate knowledge of the nonlinear dynamic systems perspective of child development and basic principles of development to aspects of the child's and/or parent's behavior.

| Areas of strength | Areas for future observation and follow-up |
| --- | --- |
| | |

*The Visit: Observation, Reflection, Synthesis for Training and Relationship Building*, by Annette Axtmann and Annegret Dettwiler.